Chinese
FOR BEGINNERS

Photo: Calligrapher at Work   (Laura DeCoppet)

Chinese
FOR BEGINNERS

Diane Wolff

Calligraphy by Jeanette Chien

BARNES & NOBLE BOOKS
A DIVISION OF HARPER & ROW, PUBLISHERS
New York, Cambridge, Philadelphia, San Francisco,
London, Mexico City, São Paulo, Singapore, Sydney

DEDICATION

For my parents, for Stanley, for Laura and Leslie

TABLE OF CONTENTS

PREFACE

    This book is designed to enable anyone to appreciate Chinese for the magnificent language it is, or to begin learning it. You can browse in it and read what interests you in any order. The English section provides background information, history of the language, discussion of calligraphy, and technical information, such as pronunciation and sentence patterns. The Chinese section contains common everyday words, their meanings, many word derivations, and the stroke order (which is the instruction for writing each character).

    The book also contains much information useful to the student engaged in formal study. It includes a chart of radicals with their meanings and pronunciations, and instructions on how to use the Chinese dictionary (with sample pages reproduced). It also contains the pronunciation chart from the Yale <u>Dictionary of Spoken Chinese</u>, and much information on the formation of characters from the works of Professor Bernhard Karlgren.

    To this author's knowledge, a book combining all this information from many different sources has not existed previously for the non-scholar. Rather, the student must discover this information for himself piecemeal over a course of several years. Thus, the author hopes it will serve as a useful companion text as well as an introductory work.

ACKNOWLEDGMENTS

In this vast field of Chinese studies, one must remain humble in the face of what one does not know, and be grateful for the wisdom of those who do know. I should especially like to thank Professor Hans Bielenstein for his interest, help, guidance and advice throughout the preparation of this book.

Mrs. Jeanette Chien, who executed the calligraphy for this book with great patience, labors and artistry, I should also like to thank. Mrs. Chien's work has been published in _Newsweek_ and now here. She is a member of the staff of the Chinese Catalogue Department of the East Asian Library of Columbia University.

I am also indebted to many of my teachers for inspiration: Professor Ainslie Embree, Mr. Charles Lo, Professor Stanley Millet, and Mr. Roger Yueh. Mr. C. C. Wang and Professor Cornelius Chang assisted me in finding a calligrapher. The interest and assistance of many friends has also been invaluable: Gerald Johnson, Bruce Wiggins, Michael McEvoy, Michael Robbins, Ke Bi-De, Mr. Daniel K. Gill, Mr. John Nicholas, and Donna Anglesano who assisted in the preparation of the first draft.

DPW
New York City, 1973

Every idea, every effort made towards better understanding
between men and peoples, every act which helps to awaken
the consciousness of world unity is of invaluable support.

quoted from a document printed after the French liberation
by Le Corbusier, the French architect, in his book, The Modulor.

ENGLISH

EUROPE AND ASIA

The romance of the Far East has captured the imagination of Europe for centuries. Asia lured the sailor, the merchant, the diplomat, the priest, the adventurer, the scholar.

Europe was infatuated with Chinese silks, paintings, calligraphy, porcelain, ivory, jade, tea and laquered ware. The infatuation caused countless caravans to cross the silk routes of the Central Asian deserts, and countless European ships to fill the Indian Ocean.

The famous Ming blue-and-white ware became the model for European porcelain. The French wanted "chinoiserie" from their furniture designers. The Italians adopted spaghetti from the Chinese and made a national cuisine of it. The Germans produced a generation of the finest Asian scholars in the world. And Chinese exploding powder enabled Europeans to improve their warfare tremendously. "It is hard to accept that the Chinese invented everything, even fettucine." (Michelangelo Antonioni, in his documentary film Jung Gwo.)

Asia passed into European literature: "Xanadu", The Accounts of Marco Polo, Lost Horizon, Passage to India. The great writers of our century have been moved by Asian themes: Mann, Yeats, Kazantzakis, Hesse. From literature and from countless films, a horde of Eastern characters floats through our collective consciousness: emperors, courtesans, eunuchs, concubines, rajas, geishas, samurai, elephant boys, ascetics, coolies, khans, empresses, warlords, sampan boys and mendicant monks. The East conjures images of palaces, intrigue, opulence, perfumes, decadence, tropical jungles, temples, lotus-blossoms, the Himalayas, the monsoon, the koto and sitar, and the intangible but ever-present spirituality written in the round Chinese faces, gentle Indian faces and the rugged Tibetan bone structure. Even the place-names breathe the exotic: Rangoon, Kuala Lumpur, Shanghai, Macao, Canton, Bengal, Peking, Lhasa, Bombay, Katmandu, Angkor Wat.

In our time, the wisdom of the East has become a light for the scientific material West: the Bhagavad Gita, yoga, Zen, Lao Tzu, I Ching, Tibetan Book of the Dead. There is an unprecedented interest in Eastern philosophy, literature, and culture. To these already enamoured Westerners, this book will seem logical. For the others and for our children, Asia will not be so distant, and Chinese not so foreign. Thus, An Easy Guide to Everyday Chinese. We are not strangers.

There is a delicacy in the Chinese
language that we shall never hope
to understand as long as we remember
our thundering hexameters. . . .
They have made language finer than
the softest silk; they have
deliberately cultivated their
sensibilities until the sound of
a petal falling may be louder
than the crash of kingdoms.
They have exalted poetry into the
place of the angels and they have
written more poetry than all the
other nations of the earth put
together.

Robert Payne, The White Pony,
viii.

CHAPTER 1

THE CHINESE LANGUAGE

The Legend of the Origin of the Chinese Script

> In the Golden Age, which was a very long time ago,
> before history, even before Chinese history, a Dragon-
> Horse came out of the Yellow River. He carried on his
> back curious symbols. The first emperor of China, Fu
> Hsi, stood on the bank. A marvelous thing happened.
> The dragon-horse revealed the symbols on his back to
> Fu Hsi, and the First Emperor copied them. Thus, he
> acquired the mystical characters which became the
> skeleton of the Book of Changes. (Retold from Karlgren,
> SSC, 32.)

This was the beginning, about 5,000 years ago.

The Chinese are the only people in the world whose
territory, language and culture have survived intact through a
5,000 year history. The language belongs to all China, and,
more than anything else is responsible for forging the cultural
unity and centrality of the Chinese--who, after all, called
themselves "the Middle Kingdom" and considered that they were
the center of the world. It is easy to see how a civilization
so ancient, so highly refined in every facet of its culture,
deemed all non-Chinese--Mongol tribesmen, Central Asian traders,
the Japanese and Westerners--"barbarians." All were received as
tribute nations, including the English at the height of the
British Empire.

To begin to know the Chinese language, it helps to have a
few simple facts which put things in full and proper perspective.

SIMPLE FACT #1: MORE PEOPLE SPEAK CHINESE THAN ANY
OTHER LANGUAGE IN THE WORLD.

There are approximately 800,000,000 Chinese. 760,000,000
actually live in China, and 95% of these speak Chinese. The
remaining 40,000,000 Chinese live in colonies around the world,
from Cuba and America in the West, to Singapore and Malaysia in
the East. In Vietnam and Korea (where people do not speak Chinese)
it has been the literary language, the language of culture and
learning, for centuries.

> Not only does Chinese exceed in
> extent the most widely spoken
> European languages, but it may
> also make good its claim to
> equal position as a civilizing
> influence. (Karlgren, SSC, 1.)

What is called Mandarin Chinese is a dialect spoken in
North China and in Peking. It is the national language of the
People's Republic of China, and one of the five languages of
the United Nations. It has been the language of the scholars
and statesmen of China for centuries. It is the dialect
introduced in this book.

Not all people speak the same Chinese however.

No one knows exactly how many dialects exist. Szchwan,
Shanghai, Canton, Amoy, and Fuchien are a few places that have
their own dialects. In some parts of China the language is
fairly homogeneous over a large area. In other places, especially
on the China south coast, the language changes every 2 or 3 miles.

These are the most archaic and divergent dialects. Sometimes it happens that people in neighboring villages cannot understand one another. The South Chinese merchant who must communicate to people of different villages but cannot master the many dialects solves the problem in an amusing fashion. He learns the essential words in English, then combines them in a purely Chinese fashion. This English words-Chinese syntax combination is called pidgin English, and is the parody of Chinese speech (no tickee, no laundry) usually found in Hollywood films. (Karlgren, SSC, 18.)

SIMPLE FACT #2: THE CHINESE SCRIPT IS READABLE AND UNDERSTANDABLE THROUGHOUT CHINA.

Though the spoken word is different, the written word is the same everywhere. Both a Peking man and a Cantonese will understand 日 means day, and 月 means moon. But a Peking man will pronounce the words r and ywe, while the Cantonese will pronounce yat and ut.

Now the original pronunciation of words has been lost, so classical texts are read in the modern pronunciation of each dialect. If the Peking man reads to the Canton man, the Canton man will not understand one word. If each man reads a text for himself, he can understand it, completely. This is because the Chinese script is not phonetic, but pictorial.

SIMPLE FACT #3: ALL CHINA POSSESSES ONE LITERARY LANGUAGE.

As a result of the separation of Chinese into a literary and colloquial language, there were two kinds of languages in China: the language of books and the language of the streets and the countryside. The language of the streets and country developed as living languages do, the language of the books always looked back to the ancient models. So, although the people were divided into dialect groups, by their spoken languages, the entire population had ONE COMMON written language.

The results of this were: a Cantonese could <u>read</u> a paper printed in Shanghai (yet he could not understand it if the Shanghai man read it in his accent). An 18th-century scholar could read the work of a Han dynasty historian. A Chinese who could read the literary language could read something written before Christ, 1,000 years ago, or yesterday. (Karlgren, SSC, 26-28.)

The fact that all dialect groups understand the Chinese script makes it possible for all China to possess one literary language, one classical literature, and one cultural consciousness.

The Chinese language holds an exalted place in Chinese culture that it is hard for Europeans and Americans to understand. Since long before Christ, China had a class of scholars who formed the most ancient modern bureaucracy in the world. Their admission to government service rested solely on their language skills: knowledge of literature, ability to compose in the literary language, and handwriting.

Stories from Chinese literature are quoted by even the most illiterate peasants. Fine handwriting is a source of pride to any Chinese, and great handwriting is considered art.

Thus, to the Chinese, language is much more than a tool of communication, it binds a vast and ancient nation, and unifies it.

SIMPLE FACT #4: CHINESE LITERATURE HAS THE LONGEST HISTORY
OF ANY LITERATURE IN THE WORLD WRITTEN IN A SINGLE LANGUAGE.

For the past 3,000 years, Chinese writers have produced
poetry, drama, stories, and novels in addition to religious
texts (the Chinese Buddhist Canon), philosophy (including the
huge Confucian and Taoist literature) and history (a Chinese
history is a complete source on the time, including biographies
of famous persons of the times, emperors, scholars, gentry, monks,
and courtesans--political and economic treatises, travelogue, and
geography).

Though the literature begins 3,000 years ago, the language
itself goes much further back. The Chinese script existed in
all its essentials more than 1,000 years before Christ.

During the Shang Dynasty (1500-1029 BC) the writing consisted
of words inscribed on pieces of tortoise shell and bone. Kings
used this method of divination to consult the ancestral spirits.
The question was carved on a tortoise shell. The shell was
reduced in thickness, a heated rod applied to the thinnest part,
and the answer was interpreted from the pattern of the cracks.
Sometimes the answer was recorded with the question.

The Chou Dynasty, China's feudal period, was the time of
both Confucius and Lao Tzu. We have only inscriptions on bronze
vessels as examples of Chinese writing from this period because
of a very dramatic incident in Chinese history. The first man
to unify China, the Emperor Chin-shr-hwang-di had to undermine

the resistance of the scholar class in order to achieve the
unification. The literati opposed his methods of government on
the grounds they differed from the classical notions of politics.
In order to achieve his political ends, the Emperor ordered the
burning of all the classical books. The <u>ideas</u> contained in the
books--the ancient principles and methods of government--were his
enemies. Some books were hidden and saved, most were lost. The
texts we do have from this period were transmitted by memory(!!)
and written down at a later date.

The Han dynasty (206-220 AD) was a great period of recon-
struction of the last books. The existing Confucian Canon dates
from the Han. From the Han to the present the literature has an
unbroken history. The Tang dynasty was noted for poetry, Sung
for metaphysics, Yuan for drama, and the Ming for the novel.

What is Chinese like as a medium of communication? This is
difficult to describe in English. Chinese is magical, an ancient
and primitive movie made of successive stills. Following its
workings is like unravelling a picture puzzle.

> The maximum of phanopoeia (throwing a
> visual image on the mind) is probably
> reached by the Chinese, due in part to
> their particular kind of written language.
> (Ezra Pound, <u>ABC</u> <u>of</u> <u>Reading</u>, 42.)

It is the difference between a character and a word.
English does not have a visual or a musical dimension, while
Chinese has both. Attempting to convey its unique qualities,
even the greatest of Chinese scholars in the West, Dr. Bernhard

Karlgren, faltered in his prose and in his comparisons with
Latin, German, English, and Indo-European, and finally lapsed
into metaphor, for poetry is the only way to describe Chinese.

> Like a set of building blocks
> Of the same size and pattern
> Chinese Words
> Are assembled
> Into the structure
> Called a sentence.
> (SSC, 15. Line division mine.)

The principle of alphabetic writing is to represent the sound of the word by analyzing the word into its constituent parts. For example, b-a-t. There is no reference to meaning. It seems quite simple and natural to us, yet it is one of the most epoch-making inventions of mankind. For the most part, the Chinese way was to represent the meaning of the word through simple pictures and groups of pictures.

Professor Bernhard Karlgren, _Sound and Symbol in Chinese_, 41.

The Egyptians finally used abbreviated pictures to represent sounds, but the Chinese still use abbreviated pictures AS pictures, that is to say, Chinese ideogram does not try to be the picture of a sound, or to be a written sign recalling a sound, but it is still the picture of a thing. . . . It means the thing or the action or quality germane to the several things that it pictures.

Ezra Pound, _ABC of Reading_.

CHAPTER 2

THE CHINESE CHARACTER

"....Those characters that more than any alphabet
conspire to make the word read the same as the thing
seen, the emotion experienced, the thought made
luminous."

(Robert Payne, The White Pony, ix.)

The basic unit of the Chinese language is one-syllable
picture-word which we call a character and which the Chinese
call dz (字).

English words are alphabet words. An alphabet is a set of
symbols which indicates the sounds of a language, and in combination, the sounds of words. An ingenious device. How an English
word works: the letters symbolize the sound of the word which
one mentally associates with the meaning. Such divergent languages
as Arabic, Hindi, Russian, French and Finnish all use alphabetic
symbols. A letter is a symbol for a sound in precisely the way
a written musical note is a symbol for a sound.

But the Chinese language is built on a totally different
concept of symbol-making. It is ideographic language, it has
picture-symbols for things and concepts. A Chinese word conveys
the sense visually. "Through the character, we arrive directly
at the sense of the word." A Chinese word is to the eye what
an English word is to the ear.

If one understands how Chinese characters are constructed, he can see them better, and see, too, the unceasing poetry of the language to its very roots.

Characters are composed in different ways. The most ancient are simply <u>drawings</u> <u>of</u> <u>objects</u>. Thousands of these old drawings are still in use, drawings of the phenomena of nature, plants and vegetables, animals, man and his attributes, ancient Chinese civilization, the parts of a house, implements of war and peace, food and drink, musical instruments, religious activities and objects. (Karlgren, SSC, 34-36.) Over an exceedingly long period of time, the primitive shapes became modified, and the round figures tended to become square. The <u>form</u> changed slightly because of technical developments in writing implements or printing methods, sometimes because certain styles of writing came into vogue. But even though the <u>form</u> changed, the <u>idea</u> represented remained the same, so that a Chinese character of 3,000 years ago is completely identifiable with the modern character.

	ANCIENT	MODERN
SUN	☉	日
MOUNTAIN		山
EYE		目
COW		牛
CORN		禾
WATER		水
TO SHOOT		射

A second way Chinese characters are composed is the creation of <u>symbols</u> <u>which</u> <u>stand</u> <u>for</u> <u>abstract</u> <u>ideas</u>. The numbers are examples of pure symbols:

一 　　　　　　二 　　　　　　三

One 　　　　　TWO 　　　　　THREE

Some others are:

上　　　<u>up</u>, <u>above</u>. Shows one line above the other, indicating the relationship "above."

下　　　<u>down</u>, <u>below</u>. Shows one line below the other.

中　　　<u>center</u>. Shows an arrow piercing a target at its center.

旦　　　<u>dawn</u>. Shows the sun over a horizontal line, rising.

Sometimes a character will use a picture of a concrete object containing an abstract idea to represent the abstract idea itself. For example, 高 is a picture of a tower (which contains the idea of height), and it means "high."

At one time, a technique called the "Loan Method" was used to get a written character. It worked like this: a character was borrowed from one word for a word which pronounced exactly the same, but had no written character. For example, "to come" and "wheat" both pronounced <u>lai</u>. There was a character for wheat 來 , because it was easy to draw. But "to come" was difficult to draw. So the character for "wheat" was borrowed to write "to come"--then "to come" was also written 來 . One had to tell from the context which was meant. There was no connection in meaning, only the sameness of sound.

The word for scorpion 萬 was borrowed to write the number 10,000 since both pronounced the same. But in this case, the original meaning, scorpion, was lost, and only means 10,000 now. Fortunately this loan method was not used too much or great confusion would have resulted.

These methods are used to create SIMPLE characters, those having only <u>one</u> picture. There are also COMPOUND characters which are more than a simple drawing or symbol. These are composed usually of several sense-elements, or one sense-element and one sound-element.

One kind of compound character is the <u>logical group</u>. To make these symbols, the Chinese combined two or more simple pictures in logical relation to each other. This is a convenient method, and there are thousands of these characters.

Some of them show two objects which possess an attribute in common. For example:

明   <u>bright</u>. Two bright objects, sun and moon.

鮮   <u>fresh</u>. Fish and sheep, which evidently had to be eaten fresh.

件   <u>individual</u>, <u>piece</u>. Man and ox, examples of individual things.

Some characters in the logical group category show several objects which, taken together, suggest an idea.

好   <u>love</u>. Woman and son, Maternal love.

寍   <u>peace</u>, <u>rest</u>. House 宀 , heart 心 , cup 皿 .

思   <u>think</u>. Heart and brain.

召   <u>condemn</u>. Mouth 口 pronouncing sentence. 刀 a sword is also shown. Amputation of various degrees was a common punishment in China.

The most common characters in this group, however, have two or more pictures which together depict action.

坐   to <u>sit</u>. Two men sitting on the ground.

見   to <u>see</u>. An eye on two legs.

焦   to <u>roast</u>. Flames beneath a bird 佳 .

算   to <u>calculate</u>. Two hands moving an abacus of bamboo.

伏   to <u>fall</u>, <u>lie</u> <u>prostrate</u>. Man acting like a dog 犬 .

Still other characters composed in a logical group show some kind of abstract quality.

男   <u>male</u>. Strength 力 in the field.

古   <u>ancient</u>. 10 十 mouths 口 , therefore, 10 generations.

隻   <u>single</u>. One (short-tailed) bird 隹 in the hand 又 .

雙   <u>double</u>. Two birds in the hand.

Some logical groups show concrete objects:

囚   <u>prisoner</u>. Man 大 in enclosure 口 .

夷   <u>barbarian</u>. Big man 大 with bow 弓 .

桑   <u>mulberry tree</u>. The tree 木 with many hands picking. Mulberry leaves have been used since ancient times in China to feed the silkworm.

There is only one drawback to this method. That is, too much ingenuity is required for the creation of each word. It is not economical in terms of creative energy. So a new method was invented. This was a combination of two methods mentioned above: the strictly pictorial representation, and the loan word. This combination had one element as a sense-indicator, and borrowed another as a phonetic indicator.

The following series will illustrate how this works:

方

This word pronounces <u>fang</u>. It means <u>square</u>.

This picture 方 appears in each of the next four words, and they too pronounce <u>fang</u>. The function of 方 in the word is to indicate the sound <u>fang</u>. Then to distinguish between all these words which sound alike, another picture indicates meaning.

紡　　fang, meaning "to spin." The sense-indicator
is silk. Loosely, "the word fang which concerns
cloth."

坊　　fang, meaning "district." The sense-indicator is
earth. Loosely, "the word fang which concerns earth."

訪　　fang, meaning "to ask." The sense indicator is
words. Thus, "the word fang which concerns words."

枋　　fang, meaning "board." The sense-indicator is
wood. "The word fang which concerns wood."

The next series is based on the character kung 工 , which
is a drawing of a carpenter's square. It means "work."

> When in archaic Chinese words were pronounced
> exactly alike, they still are pronounced alike.
> Where characters by the phonetic loan system
> were used for words which were pronounced almost,
> but not exactly, alike, the modern pronunciations
> will differ. (Professor Hans Bielenstein, in a
> letter to the author.)

功　　kung, meaning "merit," has 力 strength as its
sense-indicator.

訌　　hung, meaning "dispute," has 言 speech as its
sense-indicator.

紅　　hung, meaning "red," has 糸 silk as a sense-indicator.

扛　　kang, meaning "to carry," has 扌 hand as a
sense-indicator.

杠　　kang, meaning "bench," has 木 wood as a sense-
indicator.

江　　kung, meaning "tribute," has 氵 cowrie shell
(which was used as money) as a sense-indicator.

This is a very good method because once the new character is created, it too can be used as a phonetic or as a sense-indicator, along with another element. So the possibility of expanding the language increases greatly. For example: gu 古 meaning "ancient," when used as a phonetic with 囗 enclosure, becomes 固 gu, "solid." Now this whole word is used as a phonetic with the drawing 亻 man, and a new word 個 ge, is formed, meaning "individual."

Having considered how characters are structured, it is time to talk about how extensive a picture language can get, especially one with a long unbroken history, and a devoted scholar class. Some sources say there are half a million Chinese characters. Mathews Chinese-English Dictionary, the standard reference, gives 7,773 it is rumoured. (This author has not verified by actual count.) Many of these characters are used only in literature, and then only a few times. Thus, these huge numbers are deceiving and unnecessarily scary. The vast majority of these words do not occur in everyday speech. A good working vocabulary consists of 4,000 characters. An exceedingly literate Chinese might have at his command a vocabulary of 6,000. For the rest, you need only to know how to use a dictionary (see Ch. 4).

Now to consider how characters behave in groups. Characters, arranged in lines, make sentences. Lines of characters follow each other vertically down the page, as in the following sample from The Poetry of the Chinese by Sir John Francis Davis (Paragon Book Reprint Corp., New York, 1969).

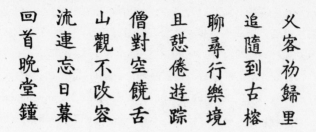

父容初歸里
追隨到古榕
聊尋行樂境
且愁倦遊踪
僧對空饒舌
山觀不改容
流連忘日暮
回首晚堂鐘

Consider the Chinese page: the vertical lines are read from right to left. Backwards, in our view.

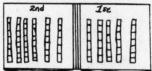

The Chinese book: the right page is read first; the left, second.

From our point of view, a Chinese book begins at the back and ends at the front.

However, concessions have been made as the result of contact with the West, and horizontal lines of characters may be found in books, especially schoolbooks, which follow the English model.

A Chinese word is really a piece of visual architecture,
like a painting, a photomontage, or a collage. Each separate
element is included in the character for a reason, either for
sense or for sound. A character means something, its construction
makes sense. (It is not just random squiggles.) Anyone can
begin to unravel the meaning and experience the composition with
a little consideration of the matter. The trick is to see the
word elements. See the logic in it. At its simplest, the
character is one picture, perhaps even one line.

人   大   天

MAN   BIG   HEAVEN

At its most complex, it is many lines making groups of
pictures, arranged in a balanced orderly composition. Some
common arrangements are as follows (using blank squares to
indicate a place where any picture may go):

TWO PICTURES:

THREE PICTURES:

FOUR PICTURES:

The following Chapter on "Radicals" (not political) tells
about the pictures which go in the squares.

To go back now for a moment to the central
thought of organic architecture, it was
Laotze, five hundred years before Jesus,
who, as far as I know, first declared that
the reality of the building consisted not in
the four walls and the roof, but inhered in
the space within, the space to be lived in.

Frank Lloyd Wright, The Future of Architecture

Chapter 3.

THE RADICAL

A Chinese word packs an emotional punch to the degree
it is understood visually by the reader. The power, the
imagery of Chinese words is locked in pictures. So, it is
extremely important to be able to see them. Learning radicals
then, one really begins to understand Chinese. Radicals are
the 214 basic drawings which all Chinese words are made of.

Why are the radicals the key to the language? They are the
roots. To analyze the meaning of a character, break it down to
its roots, into radicals. To find a character in the dictionary,
break it down to its roots, into radicals. To find a character
in the dictionary, break it down into radicals. To properly
write a character, balance its radicals.

Every radical is a drawing of an animal, man, man-made
object, nature object, or a simple symbol. The meaning is
constant. In Chinese, 木 always means tree, 扌 always
means hand, and 日 always means sun.

RADICALS CAN STAND ALONE AS WORDS.

心

Radical 61. Heart.
From the ancient drawing .

人

Radical 9. Man.
A man walking.

emphasizing the fifty most common forms

	28 山	29 又	46	66	91 片	92 牙	110 矛	111 矢	130 月	154 貝	170 阝	192 鬯	193 高
1 一	1 丨	3	30	47 巛 川	48 工	49 己	68 斗	69 斤	93 牛	112 肉	131 貝	155 赤	171 隶	11
3 丶	4 丿	5 乙	31 口	50 巾	70 方	71 旡 无	94 牛	113 禾 示	114 肉	132 自	133 至	156 走	157 隹	172 佳	194 魚
2 二	7 二	8 亠	31 口	51 干	52 幺	72 日	95 犬	96 王	115 舛	134 臼	135 舌	158 足	168 身	173 雨	195 鳥 166
9 人	10 人 儿	32 土 士	53 广	73 曰	74 月	97 穴	116 立	118 竹	140 艸 艹	141 血	159 車	176 面	177 革	178 韋	197 鹵 198 鹿
12 八 八	13 冂	33 士	34 夂	54 廾	55 廾	75 木	98 瓜	99 甘	119 米	142 虍	161 辰	162 虫	180 音	182 風	181 黑 200 麻 麻
14 一	16 几	17 凵	35 夂	36 夕	56 弋	57 弓	76 欠	100 瓦	101 生 用	120 糸	144 行	146 西	163 辵	183 飛	184 首 205 鼎 206
18 刂 刀	38 大	39 女	58 彐	59 彡	77 止	78 歹	102 田	145 衣	164 酉	165 采	185 首	207 鼓 209 鼠			14
19 力	40 子	61 彳	85	104	121 缶	7	166 里	8	186 香	19	209 鼻 210 齊			15
20 勹	21 匕	41 寸	42 小	62 戈	63 戶 户	106 白	107 皮	124 羽 羽	125 老 耂	149 角	167 金 釒	168 長 镸	187	211 齒
22 匸	23 匚	43 尢 尢	44 尸	45 屮	65 支	67 文	108 皿	128 耳	129 聿	150 谷	151 豆	169 門 門	188 骨 189 高	212 龍 213 龜
24 十	25 卜	26 卩 巳	27 厂	87	88 父	89 爻	90 爿	131 臣	152 豸	153 豕	190 髟 191 鬥	17	214 龠

Calligraphy by Maurice Tseng, IFEL 1959

Radical 85. Water.

Radical 86. Fire.

Or the radical can be used with a complement.   The
radical is always the sense-indicator. The complement (one or
more pictures) is usually a phonetic, but it may also elaborate
the meaning.

Radicals and complements are arranged many different
ways in Chinese characters. Side-by-side and above-and-below
are the most common. Both will be arranged in that striking
asymmetrical balance which so delights the Chinese.

Many radicals are abbreviated when they do not stand alone
as a character. The abbreviation is for looks and for space.

Fire, when it appears at the bottom of a character (as
in 黑) is written 灬 . Man 人 , when it appears at the
side of a character (as in 個) is written: 亻 .   Water
水 , when it appears at the side of a character (as in 江)
is written 氵 .   Heart 心 , when it appears at the side
of a character, as in 慢 is written 忄 .

There are not too many of these abbreviations, and they
appear in the radical list at the end of this chapter.

Following, some examples of the arrangements of radicals
and complements in characters:

SIDE BY SIDE

糸

One Picture. Silk.

紅

Two Pictures. Red.

紹

Three Pictures. Connect.

縵

Four Pictures. Silk Thread.

ABOVE AND BELOW

恐

Two balanced above Heart.

問

Two surrounding Mouth.

藥

Three above, Tree (木) below.

Following are a few examples of discovering the meaning
of characters by breaking them down into radicals.

忠

The word jung meaning loyal.

The symbol for center, jung 中 , is the phonetic here.
The heart radical is below. A loose poetic translation of
this character is: the heart's being in the center, thus
steadfast, thus loyal. Arriving at the meaning of words by
several extensions is common in the translation of classical

texts. This is one reason why some scholars say a full rendering of Chinese into English is impossible, but other scholars disagree. This visual architecture builds suggestion and association into words which is inconceivable to people raised on alphabet language. This kind of sensory echo, association whirlpool is what James Joyce, e. e. cummings, and the French Symbolist poets were trying to achieve in alphabet language.

坐

Dzwo, <u>To</u> <u>Sit</u>.

Earth 土 , is the radical here. 从 are two men <u>sitting</u> on the earth, a drawing of the activity.

信

Syin, <u>Sincerity</u>.

A man 亻 , standing beside his word 言 , which implies faithfulness, sincerity.

算

Swan, <u>To</u> <u>Calculate</u>.

Bamboo 竹 , is the radical because the abacus, the calculating instrument is made of bamboo. Then, a primitive picture of an abacus 目 , and two hands 廾 (𠬞 in the ancient version). Thus, "two hands working on an abacus made of bamboo" is "to calculate."

Following is a list of the 214 Radicals by number
as they appear in the Chinese dictionary. Familiarize yourself
with them, and the squiggles will start to make sense. Also
included is the meaning, the Chinese pronunciation, abbreviations
and examples of characters in which they appear. They are listed
according to number of strokes, those with the least number
first. A little familiarity with the list and radicals become
second nature.

THE 214 RADICALS

(Arranged by Number of Strokes)

Radical Number	Radical	Pronounces	Meaning	Example
ONE STROKE				
1	一	yī	one	七
2	丨	gwǔn	in calligraphy, a down stroke	中
3	丶	jǔ	a dot	丸
4	丿	pyē	a stroke curving left	乂
5	乙	yǐ	one (bent)	九
6	亅	chywé	a hooked stroke	了
TWO STROKES				
7	二	èr	two	井
8	亠	tóu	above, cover	亢
9	亻, 人	rén	a man (erect)	今
10	儿	rén	a man (going)	元
11	入	rù	enter	全
12	八	bā	eight	六
13	冂	chyǔng	borders	回
14	冖	mì	to cover	冗
15	冫	bīng	ice	冬
16	几	chī	table, stool	処
17	凵	kǎn	receptacle	凶
18	刂, 刀	dāu	knife	分
19	力	lì	strength	加
20	勹	bāu	wrap	勿
21	匕	bǐ	spoon, ladle	化
22	匚	fāng	basket	匡
23	匸	syǐ	box	匹
24	十	shŕ	ten	千
25	卜	bǔ	to divine	卞
26	卩, 㔾	jyé	seal, stamp	印
27	厂	hàn	a cliff	厄

Radical Number	Radical	Pronounces	Meaning	Examples
28	厶	sz̄	private	厷
29	又	yòu	also; a hand	收

THREE STROKES

Radical Number	Radical	Pronounces	Meaning	Examples
30	口	kǒu	mouth	可
31	囗	wéi	enclosure	囚
32	土	tǔ	earth	在
33	士	shr̀	scholar	壬
34	夂	jr̄	step forward	夆
35	夂,夊	swēi	walk slowly	夏
36	夕	syì	evening	外
37	大	dà	great	太
38	女	nyǔ	female	奴
39	子	dz̄	child, son	孔
40	宀	myán	roof	完
41	寸	tswùn	inch	寺
42	小	syǎu	small	少
43	尢,兀,尣	wāng	lame, crooked	尤
44	尸	shr̄	a corpse	尺
45	屮	chè	a sprout	芔
46	山	shān	hill	岐
47	巛,川	chwān	a stream	巡
48	工	gūng	work	左
49	己	jǐ	self	巴
50	巾	jīn	napkin	帀
51	干	gān	shield	平
52	幺	yāu	little, fine	幼
53	广	yǎn	roof, shelter	庀
54	廴	yǐn	move on	廷
55	廾	gǔng	folded hands	弁

Radical Number	Radical	Pronounces	Meaning	Examples
56	弋	yì	shoot	式
57	弓	gūng	bow	引
58	⺕	jì	pig's head	归
59	彡	shān	feathery	形
60	彳	chr	left step	彷

FOUR STROKES

Radical Number	Radical	Pronounces	Meaning	Examples
61	忄,心,小	syīn	heart	必
62	戈	gē	a spear	戊
63	户,戸	hù	door, family	所
64	扌,手	shǒu	hand	扎
65	支	jr̄	branch, prop	支
66	攵,攴	pū	tap, rap	收
67	文	wén	literature	斉
68	斗	dǒu	a peck	料
69	斤	jīn	axe, catty	斥
70	方	fāng	square	榜
71	无,旡	wú	not	既
72	日	r̀	sun, day	旦
73	曰	ywē	to say	曲
74	月	ywē	moon, month	有
75	木	mù	wood, tree	本
76	欠	chyàn	owe	次
77	止	jř	to stop	正
78	歹	dǎi	bad	死
79	殳	shū	pole-ax, kill	殺
80	毋	wú	do not	每
81	比	bǐ	compare	毖
82	毛	máo	hair (on body)	毡
83	氏	shr̀	clan	氏

Radical Number	Radical	Pronounce	Meaning	Examples
84	气	chì	air, breath	氣
85	氵, 水, 氺	shwěi	water	永
86	火, 灬	hwǒ	fire	灰
87	爫, 爪	jǎu	claws	爭
88	父	fǔ	father	爺
89	爻	yáu	intertwine	爽
90	爿	chwáng	frame, bed	牀
91	片	pyàn	a slip, a strip	版
92	牙	yá	tooth	雅
93	牜, 牛	nyóu	ox	牧
94	犭, 犬	chywán	dog	狗

FIVE STROKES

95	玄, 玄	sywán	dark, deep	兹
96	王, 玉	yu	gem, jade	珍
97	瓜	gwā	melon	瓢
98	瓦	wǎ	tile	瓶
99	甘	gān	sweet	甜
100	生	shēng	produce	產
101	用	yùng	use	甫
102	田	tyán	field	男
103	疋	pǐ	roll of cloth	靈
104	疒	nì	sick	疾
105	癶	bwǒ	legs spread out	登
106	白	bái	white	百
107	皮	pí	skin	皰
108	皿	mǐn	dish	盃
109	目, 罒	mù	eye	看
110	矛	máu	lance	矜
111	矢	shř	arrow	矣

Radical Number	Radical	Pronounces	Meaning	Examples
112	石	shŕ	stone	石工
113	示 示 礻	shŕ	reveal	祖
114	内	rŏu	beast's track	禺
115	禾 禾	hé	growing grain	私
116	穴	sywè	cave, hold	窍
117	立	lì	to stand	站

SIX STROKES

118	竹 竹	jú	bamboo	笋
119	米	mĭ	kernels, rice	精
120	糸 糸	mì	silk	約
121	缶	fŏu	pottery, earthenware	缸
122	皿 网 罒	wăng	a net	署
123	羊	yáng	sheep	羚
124	羽	yŭ	quill feathers	習
125	老 耂	lău	old	耆
126	而	ér	and, yet	耑
127	耒	lěi	a plough	耕
128	耳	ěr	ear	耶
129	聿	yù	stylus	肆
130	月 肉	ròu	flesh	助
131	臣	chén	official	卧
132	自	dz̀	self, from	臭
133	至	jr̀	reach	致
134	臼	jyòu	mortar	舅
135	舌	shé	tongue	舍
136	舛	chwăn	opposed to	舞
137	舟	jōu	boat	航
138	艮	gèn	a limit, perverse or hard	良
139	色	sè	color	艳
140	艹 艹 艹	tsău	grass, herbs	花

Radical Number	Radical	Pronounces	Meaning	Examples
141	虎	hu	tiger	虎
142	虫	chúng	insect	姐
143	血	syě	blood	衄
144	行	syíng	go, do	街
145	衤衣,衣	yī	clothes	裡
146	襾 (西)	syà, syì	a cover, west	要

SEVEN STROKES

147	見	jyàn	see, perceive	規
148	角	jywé	horn, angle	解
149	言,言	yán	words	話
150	谷	gǔ	gully, ravine	俗
151	豆	dòu	platter, bean	頭
152	豕	shr	pig	豚
153	豸	jài	footless	豹
154	貝	bèi	cowrie shell	貞
155	赤	chr̀	red, bare	赦
156	走	dzǒu	walk	赴
157	足,足	dzú	foot, enough	跑
158	身	shén	body	躬
159	車	chē	cart	軍
160	辛	syīn	pungent	碎
161	辰	chen	time	農
162	辶,辶,辵	jwǒ	run and stop	近
163	阝,邑	yì	city, district	郊
164	酉	yǒu	new wine, ripe	酒
165	采	byàn	to separate	釉
166	里	lǐ	Chinese mile, village	重

EIGHT STROKES

167	金	jīn	gold, metal	錢

Radical Number	Radical	Pronounces	Meaning	Examples
168	長,長	cháng	long	長
169	門	mén	door	間
170	阝,阜	fǒu	a mound, plenty	防
171	隶	dài	reach to	隸
172	隹	jwēi	short-tailed bird	隻
173	雨,雨	yǔ	rain	雪
174	青,青,青	chīng	nature colors--blue, green, etc.	靚
175	非	fēi	wrong, not	靠

NINE STROKES

176	面	myàn	face, surface	靦
177	革	gé	rawhide	靳
178	韋	wéi	leather	偉
179	韭	jyǒu	leeks	韮
180	音	yīn	sound	韶
181	頁	yè	the head, a page	順
182	風	fēng	the wind	颺
183	飛	fēi	to fly	飛
184	食,食	shŕ	to eat	飯
185	首	shǒu	head	馗
186	香	syāng	fragrance	馥

TEN STROKES

187	馬	mǎ	horse	嗎
188	骨	gǔ	bone	體
189	高	gāu	high	稿
190	髟	byāu	bushy human hair	髮
191	鬥	dòu	to fight	鬧
192	鬯	chàng	fragrant sacrificial wine	鬯
193	鬲	lì	three-legged incense cauldron	融
194	鬼	gwěi	spirits of the dead	魄

Radical Number	Radical	Pronounces	Meaning	Example
ELEVEN STROKES				
195	魚	yú	fish	鯉
196	鳥	nyǎu	long-tailed birds	鳴
197	鹵	lǔ	rock salt	鹹
198	鹿	lù	deer	麟
199	麥	mài	wheat	麩
200	麻	má	hemp	麿
TWELVE STROKES				
201	黃	hwáng	yellow	黃
202	黍	shǔ	glutinous millet	黏
203	黑	hēi	black	點
204	黹	jr	embroidery	黻
THIRTEEN STROKES				
205	黽	měng	frog or toad	蠅
206	鼎	dǐng	tripod	鼐
207	鼓	gǔ	drum	鼕
208	鼠	shǔ	rodent	鼢
FOURTEEN STROKES				
209	鼻	bí	nose	鼾
210	齊	chí	even	齎
FIFTEEN STROKES				
211	齒	chǐ	front teeth	齡
SIXTEEN STROKES				
212	龍	lúng	dragon	龐
213	龜	gwei	tortoise	龜
SEVENTEEN STROKES				
214	龠	ywè	flute, pipes	龢

CHAPTER 4

CHINESE SOUNDS AND SYLLABLES: PRONUNCIATION

Extraordinary fact: Chinese is a completely monosyllabic
language. This means: Every Chinese character has a one-
syllable sound. These syllables have been formed the same way
for a thousand years. This produces some startling effects in
Chinese speech. Its clipped rocking quality, the incredible
number of rhymes, the small variety of sounds and a great many
words which pronounce exactly alike.

If English were monosyllabic, our sentences would sound
like this: rain hard, man want come in, from far town, need
food, all wet, can we give roof? Chinese sounds like this:
jeige ren yau jinlai, shr tsung yuan chenglide, keyi gei ta
chrfanma?

English words are freewheeling weddings of letters. Chinese
syllables are strict unions formed according to ancient patterns.
English has infinite numbers of possible syllables. Chinese
has a very limited number--about 420 in Peking Mandarin. English
can have clusters of consonants at the beginning, middle, and
end of words, and a great variety of vowel combinations. Chinese
syllables must be composed of a CONSONANT-VOWEL (gu, ba, ni, wo,
hai, de) or CONSONANT-VOWEL-CONSONANT (fen, han, cheng, gen,
nin) or VOWEL-CONSONANT (an, er). And only certain consonants
and certain vowels can be used.

The Chinese have three categories of sounds: initials, finals, and vowels (also a few "semi-vowels").

The initial sound must be simple and single. There are no clusters of letters such as the English scr-, thr-, pl-. Only 21 letters can begin a Chinese syllable:

f-	p-	ch-	ts-
l-	t-	j-	dz-
m-	k-	sy-	yw-
r-	b-	sh-	y-
s-	d-	h-	w-
g-			

Only three consonants are permitted to end a syllable: -n, -ng, -r.

The vowels are:

-a	-ei	-u	-e
-ai	-0	-z	-i
-au	-ou	-r	

There are also three semi-vowels: -y-, -w-, and -yw- (sounds like u in ruin). These semi-vowels fall between an initial and a vowel, as in hwa, sywan, or chyu.

These 38, in combination, make the sum of possible sounds in Chinese. This particular limitation is a great help to anyone learning to speak the language. It makes things very simple. Chinese sounds, oddly enough, are natural to English speaking people. Only a few sounds do not appear in our language. Most consonants pronounce exactly the same. The vowels must be learned carefully. To give the reader a solid reference, the section on pronunciation from the Yale Dictionary of Spoken Chinese is included here.

It is a clear precise guide and will serve well should
the reader be in doubt about pronouncing any word in this book.

A SHORT DIGRESSION INTO THE
HISTORY OF CHINESE SOUNDS TO
EXPLAIN THE PHENOMENON OF TONES.

The consonant-vowel-(optional) consonant pattern which was
formed by 500 A.D. has been the Chinese rule for 1500 years.
Ancient Chinese had series of sounds like this: ga, gat, gap,
gak, gan, gam, gang (varying only the final).

The rich vocabulary of ancient Chinese reflected the fact
that the culture was very old and highly civilized. This poverty
of sounds had to accommodate a lush profusion of words. The
result: homophones, scores of them. (Homophones are words which
pronounce the same but are written differently and have different
meanings.)

> This homophony was considerably
> increased by the fact that Chinese in
> the course of its evolution, as far
> back as it can be traced, has always
> tended to sound simplification. (SSC, 16.)

For example: at one time, ancient Mandarin simply dropped
most of its final sounds. When the finals were dropped, all the
words in this series:

> Ga, song
> Gap, frog
> Gat, cut
> Gag, each

then pronounced the same, Ga. Today, they still pronounce the
same, but the syllable now has the sound Ge. The point is that
thousands of words having different sounds, all at once, had

the same sound.

More homophones were produced when all the words ending in -m changed to an -n ending. In addition to all the words which already ended in -n. The ancient word for south, <u>nam</u> (as in Vietnam), became <u>nan</u>, and became indistinguishable in pronunciation from <u>nan</u>, difficult.

The vowel elements were simplified too. The ancient language had diverse vowel sounds: <u>li</u>, fox; <u>lye</u>, leave; and <u>lyei</u>, ceremony. The modern language has one syllable for all, <u>li</u>.

Thus, the modern dialects have <u>fewer sounds</u> than the ancient because of this strong tendency to simplify. And more words have the <u>same</u> sound in modern Chinese. Peking Mandarin has 420 syllables. <u>420 syllables contain every word in the entire Chinese language</u>. Thus, the monosyllabic quality, the strict syllable formation and the sound simplification cause the striking Chinese sound.

Just to show the effect on the sound of Chinese, here is a series of "rhymes" with the same vowel and final sound, with only <u>the initial</u> varied:

jeng	beng	cheng
peng	feng	seng
heng	sheng	reng
deng	geng	teng
leng	dzeng	meng
tseng	neng	weng

Thus, a hint of the limitations and beauties of Chinese poetry. While, on the other hand, our multiple syllable English words of every conceivable sound grouping are capable of forming the charge of Milton's cadences.

A small dictionary of common usage, containing only the most simple words, has about 4200 entries. That gives an average of 10 words per syllable. But the words are not evenly distributed. The sound i (ee) has 69 words listed, and shr has 59, but rwun has only 2.

The question which now occurs to every Westerner is: HOW DO YOU TELL THE DIFFERENCE BETWEEN ALL THESE WORDS WHICH PRONOUNCE EXACTLY ALIKE? The answer: BY THE TONES.

Tones came about to distinguish between the homophones, so that people could understand one another when speaking. Two identical syllables sound differently when pronounced on different musical notes. Tones distinguish between spoken words which sound the same, just as radicals differentiate between written words which sound the same.

SOUNDS

1. Symbols Used

In this Dictionary the sounds of Chinese are indicated by the following letters and other symbols:

Representing *consonant sounds*: b, ch, d, dz, f, g, h, j, k, l, m, n, ng, p, r, s, sh, sy, t, ts, w, y, yw.

Representing *vowel sounds*: a, ai, au, e, ee, ei, o, ou, i, u, r, z.

Representing *tones*: accent marks put over a letter, as follows: neutral tone a (no accent mark), first tone ā, second tone á, third tone ă, fourth tone à.

Representing *stress* (or *loudness* or *prominence*): a raised tick (') placed before a syllable.

In the interest of economy, some of the letters or groups of letters, or other symbols, are used to represent more than one sound, but only when (1) the sounds are similar and (2) they occur only in mutually exclusive environments, so that the conditions under which a single symbol represents one or another sound can be clearly defined.

2. Consonants at the Beginning of a Syllable

In the following, the first column lists a symbol, the second column lists the conditions under which that symbol represents the sound described in the third column, and the fourth column gives examples. The order is as follows: f, l, m, n, r, s, w, y, p, t, k, b, d, g, ts, dz, ch, j, sy, sh, h, ng, yw; this order is used because it puts the most familiar sounds first and groups together those which represent similar difficulties.

Symbol	Conditions	Description	Examples	
f	everywhere	as in English fun.	fěn	"powder"
l	everywhere	as in English low.	lòu	"to leak"
m	everywhere	as in English my.	mài	"to sell"
n	everywhere	as in English now.	nǎu	"to annoy"
r	everywhere	as in English run, but with no rounding of the lips.	rén	"person"

(The main differences between the Chinese r- and the general American r- are (1) that the lips are never rounded except when the r is followed by a vowel requiring rounding, such as rwǎn "be soft"; (2) that there is no curling of the tip of the tongue backward. The whole front surface of the tongue is pulled backward and pushed up, still flat, close to the roof of the mouth.)

s	everywhere	as in English sigh.	sài	"to compete"
w	everywhere	as in English way.	wèi	"because of"
y	everywhere	as in English yeah.	yá	"tooth"

(But note that yw is treated as a special symbol)

p	everywhere	as in English pie, but with a stronger puff of breath.	pài	"to appoint"
t	everywhere	as in English tie, but with a stronger puff of breath.	tài	"too, very"
k	everywhere	as in English kite, but with a stronger puff of breath.	kāi	"to open"

(The puff of breath or "aspiration" which follows the first consonant of the English words pie, tie, kite can be tested by holding a small slip of very light-weight paper before the lips as the words are spoken. The paper will flutter slightly just as the first consonant ends. For the Chinese sounds written with the same letters, the paper should flutter considerably more.)

b	everywhere	as in English buy, but without voicing; or as English p in pie, but without any puff of breath.	bài	"to worship"
d	everywhere	as in English die, but without voicing; or as English t in tie, but without any puff of breath.	dài	"to put on"

| g | everywhere | as in English guy, but without voicing; or as English k in kite, but without any puff of breath. | gài | "to cover" |

(There are three ways to acquire these sounds: (1) Practice with the slips of paper as suggested above, and try to say the words so that the paper does not flutter at all. (2) Hold your hands over your ears and say the word buy, die, guy; you will hear a buzz that begins with the initial consonant and continues throughout. Then try to say the words so that the buzz does not begin until after the initial consonant. (3) Say the words spy, sty, sky with the slip of paper, and notice that it does not flutter. Take the initial s- away and try to say the p, t, and k in just the same way, without causing the paper to flutter.)

| ts | everywhere | like the ts-h of English it's high with the initial i left off. | tsài | "vegetable" |

| dz | everywhere | like the ts of English it's I with the initial i left off. | dzài | "again" |

(Pretend you are a phonograph record, with the expressions it's high and it's I recorded on it; put the needle down just past the place where the i of it's high or the i of it's I is recorded. The difference between ts and dz is comparable to the difference between p and b, t and d, or k and g as described earlier.)

ch	(1) before i, y, yu or yw	much as in English cheat, but with the tip of the tongue held down behind the lower front teeth.	chí chyán chyù chywán	"air" "money" "to go" "whole"
	(2) elsewhere	a cross between true and choose—as though we said chrue instead of true.	chá chū	"tea" "exit"
j	(1) before i, y, yu or yw	like Chinese ch in the same conditions, except with no puff of breath.	jí jyàu jyù jywé	"remember" "be called" "according to" "absolutely"
	(2) elsewhere	like Chinese ch in the same conditions, except with no puff of breath.	jū ja	"pig" "to fry"

(The most important thing in correctly pronouncing ch and j when not before i, y, yu, or yw is to draw the tip of the tongue back and up to the roof of the mouth; avoid scrupulously making a sound like the English ch in chase or chair, or j in Jack or jump, which are made with the tongue much farther forward in the mouth. Note the difference between the ch type of sound, which has a puff of breath, and the j type, which does not.)

| sy | everywhere | much as in English she, but with the tip of the tongue held down behind the lower front teeth, and without any rounding of the lips. | syí
syàu | "west"
"small" |

sh	everywhere	a cross between the **sh** of **shoe** and the **shr** of **shrew**, with the tongue drawn well back and up.	shū	"book"
			shǎu	"few"
h	everywhere	either like the English **h** in **how**, or with friction at the back of the mouth, as in German a**ch**.	hǎu	"OK"
			hú	"lake"

(Most speakers of Chinese vary between these two; either is acceptable, but to use the English h sound constantly may make your pronounciation occasionally unpleasant to Chinese ears.)

ng	everywhere (occurs only when the preceding syllable ends in **ng**.)	like the **ng** of **singer** (not like the **ng** of **finger**.)	bùsyíng nga!	"It won't do!"
yw	everywhere	the sound of y as in **yes** and w as in **won't** pronounced at the same time.	ywè	"month"
			ywǎn	"far"

(The tongue is in the position for y, but the lips are rounded as for w. Sometimes the sound starts just slightly before the lips are rounded, but the two are simultaneous.)

3. Semi-Vowel in the Middle of a Syllable

The following semi-vowels occur after a consonant and before a vowel, with or without another consonant following the last vowel. There are three of them, w, y and yw.

w	everywhere	like the English u in **suave** or **quality**.	hwā	"flower"
			lwàn	"mess"
			hwáng	"yellow"
y	(1) before vowel other than **e, u.**	Like the English y in **Ilya**, and the **i** in **California.**	lyǎ	"two"
			dyàn	"electricity"
	(2) before **e.**	(See #5 under vowel e (2))		
	(3) before **u.**	(See #5 under vowel u (3))		
yw	(1) before vowel other than **e.**	like the French u in **nuance.**	jywǎn	"to roll"
			sywǎn	"to elect"
			chywǎn	"fist"
	(2) before **e.**	(See #5 under vowel e (2))		

4. Consonants at the End of a Syllable

The following consonants occur at the ends of syllables: They are n, ng, r and ngr.

n	(1) except as mentioned under (2).	like the English n in **can.**	wén	"smell"
			tán	"converse"
	(2) when the next syllable begins with **y.**	the tongue does not quite reach the roof of the mouth, and the preceding vowel is slightly nasalized.	tán yi tán	"converse a bit"

ng	everywhere	like the English ng in sing or singer (not like the ng in finger).	táng háng húng	"candy, sugar" "trade" "red"
r	everywhere	like the English r in bar, fur.	wár fèr	"to play" "portion"

(In many varieties of English, r's after a vowel are not pronounced. Whatever variety of English you speak, be sure to pronounce the r in Chinese; but don't trill or roll it; make an English r-sound, not a French or German r-sound.)

ngr	everywhere	the back of the tongue does not reach the roof of the mouth for the ng; the vowel is strongly nasalized; r as described above.	héngr	"horizontal stroke"

5. <u>Vowels</u>

The vowels are a, ai, au, e, ee, ei, o, ou, i, u, z, and r.

a	(1) except as detailed below.	like the English a in father or ma.	mǎ	"horse"
	(2) between y and n.	like the English a in hand.	yān dyàn	"smoke" "electricity"
	(3) between yw and n.	like the English a in bat, but variable; some speakers make it like (1), some like (2).	ywàn chywán	"court" "altogether"
	(4) between w and ng.	like (1) or like the English o in long.	hwāng	"nervous"
ai	everywhere	like the English ai in aisle.	pài	"to appoint"
au	everywhere	like the English au in umlaut or Faust.	lǎu	"old"
e	(1) except as specified below.	about like the English u in but or huh.	hē chē hěn	"to drink" "cart" "very"

(When final in the syllable, this sound often begins with the back of the tongue drawn back and up toward the roof of the mouth, like the oo in book without the lips rounded; but it then glides from this to the sound described above.)

	(2) after sy, y or yw, final in the syllable.	like the English e in met or eah or yeah.	yě ywè syè	"also" "month" "to thank"
ei	everywhere	like the English ei in reign.	pèi	"to match"
ee	everywhere	the first e is as above, depending on the preceding sound; the second as (1) above.	héer gěer	"small box" "song"
o	everywhere	like the English u in urn.	wǒ	"I"

| ou | everywhere | like the English ow in know. | hòu | "behind" |

| i | (1) final in the syllable. | like the English ee in see. | mǐ | "rice grain" |
| | (2) not final in the syllable. | like the English i in pin. | mín | "people" |

(Consonants before i are often pronounced with a little y-glide after them, as though one said myín instead of mín.)

u	(1) final and not after sy, y.	like the English oo in moon.	wǔ shū	"five" "book"
	(2) followed by a consonant and not after sy, y.	like the English oo in book.	húng	"red"
	(3) after sy, y.	like the English oo in moon and the ee in see pronounced simultaneously.	syù syún yǔ yún	"to continue" "to look for" "rain" "to ship"

(The tongue is in the ee-position, and the lips are rounded as for oo. This is the same position as described already for the consonant sound yw.)

| z | everywhere | like the English oo in look pronounced without rounding the lips; the throat is tense and the back of the tongue is held down tightly. | dż tsż sż | "word" "jab" "four" |

(This sound occurs only after the consonants dz, ts, and s. The consonant dz and the vowel z are transcribed as dz when combined.)

| r | everywhere | like the middle-western American English ir in shirt, or ur in hurt, fur; something like French je when it stands alone. | r̃ chr̃ jr̃ shr̃ | "sun" "to eat" "straight" "is" |

(This sound occurs only after the consonants r, ch, j, and sh. When the consonant r and the vowel r are combined, only one r is written.)

6. Tones and Stress

A syllable uttered in isolation has one of four basic *tonal contours* or *tones*. In longer expressions, the individual syllables may have one of a number of allotones, all related to that particular one of the four which the same syllable has in isolation. Syllables also may have no definite tonal contour at all. These last are called *toneless* or *neutral tone* syllables, and are written without any tone mark.

The distinctiveness of the tonal contours described below depends on the loudness or prominence of the syllable in question: more distinct when louder, less distinct when softer.

Tone	Symbol	Conditions	Description	Examples	
first	ˉ (ā)	everywhere	high, level, sometimes	gāu	"high"

			cut off sharply at the end.	tsā	"to scrape"
second	(á)	everywhere	relatively high, rising with increasing loudness; often cut off sharply at the end.	rén báu ná tsúng	"person" "thin" "to take" "from"
third	(ǎ)	(1) stressed at end of a phrase (before pause).	low in pitch, rising at the end, and gradually less loud.	mǎ kǔ yǒu hǎu	"horse" "bitter" "there is" "OK"
		(2) before another syllable with third tone (ˇ).	mid-low, rising, sometimes not distinguishable from second tone (´).	wǒ yǒu becomes wó yǒu hǎikǒu becomes háikǒu	"I have" "seaport"

(Sometimes the tone of the second syllable becomes neutral. As dásau "clean up" derived from dǎsǎu.)

		(3) otherwise	low, with no rise.	yǒu rén mǎchē	"there are people" "horse cart"
fourth	(à)	(1) stressed	falling from high to mid-low or low.	rè hàu	"hot" "number"
		(2) unstressed	falling but often only slightly, and from whatever level is reached by the preceding syllable; if none, from mid-high.	shàngsyàu kànbujyàn	"colonel" "can't see"
neutral	none	everywhere	short, middle pitch.	tāde rénde wǒde hwàide dehwà	"his" "people's" "mine" "bad ones" "in case"

Stress means the relative degree of loudness or prominence of syllables when they are joined together. In Chinese, stress follows the scheme below:

(ˇ stands for any one of the four tones)

Two-syllable elements

1. ˉˉ means stress is on the second syllable, both tones pronounced.

2. ˉˉ means stress is on the first syllable, the second syllable neutral.

3. ' ˉˉ means stess is on the first syllable, both tones pronounced.

Three-syllable elements

1. ˉˉˉ means stress is on the last syllable, all tones pronounced.

2. ˉˉˉ means stress is on the second syllable, the last syllable neutral.

3. In other cases, three-syllable elements should be pronounced according to stress marks indicated.

In every case, elements of more than three syllables should be pronounced according to stress marks indicated.

7. Changes of Sound

1. **Occasional changes.** Some elements in Chinese vary in pronunciation without any correlated change in meaning. The most frequent case of this is when an element within certain compounds or contexts loses its tone: bùhǎu "not good", with bù "not"; but hǎubuhǎu "is it good?" with bu toneless. Cases of this kind are properly indicated in the body of the Dictionary. Some elements occur in all possible contexts with either of two tones, or even sometimes with any of three tones.

2. **Regular Changes.** The element -r differs from most constituent elements of expressions in Chinese in that it is joined onto the previous syllable as part of that same syllable instead of constituting a syllable in itself. The merging of a syllable with suffixed -r calls for certain systematic changes in the vowels and consonants of the original first syllable; the tone is not affected. The following table shows the changes made:

Syllables ending in:	When adding -r become:	Examples:	
-a	-ar	hwā	: hwǎr
-an	-ar	hwǎn	: hwǎr
-ai	-ar	hwái	: hwár
-au	-aur	hǎu	: hǎur
-ang	-angr	háng	: hángr
-e	-er	gě	: gěr
	-eer	gě	: gěer

(Speakers differ in the latter usage. With the first and second tones transcription using two e's has generally been used; with the third and fourth tones transcription using one e has been generally used.)

-o	-oer	wǒ	: wǒer
	-or	wǒ	: wǒr

(Speakers differ here also; but all the forms are used.)

-en	-er	gěn	: gěr
-ei	-er	swèi	: swèr
-ou	-our	gǒu	: gǒur
-eng	-engr	héng	: héngr
-i	-yer	dí	: dyèr
(yi)	(yer)	(yí	: yèr)
-in	-yer	jín	: jyěr
(yin)	(yer)	(yǐn	: yěr)
-ing	-ingr	bǐng	: bǐngr
-u	-ur	shù	: shùr
-ung	-ungr	húng	: húngr

CHAPTER 5

ABOUT TONES

Now for the music. The Chinese used pitch to resolve
the difficulties caused by the small number of syllables the
language had. When it evolved into a tonal language, it became
the perfect language: a poetic picture-medium with built-in
music.

A tone is a musical note a Chinese word is always sung on
or pronounced with. As Professor Karlgren puts it:

> "In every Chinese word, there is inherent
> a certain melody and words otherwise
> phonetically identical can be distinguished
> by their different melodies."

There are four tones in Mandarin Chinese. (Cantonese has
nine.) These tones are precise enough to be expressed as musical
notes. These notes and an approximate English equivalent are
given to help the reader get the correct sound, until he can
have a Chinese speaker pronounce them for him. Pitch varies from
person to person, male voices being generally deeper than female
voices.

1.   The High Tone (Or First Tone)
     Said like the ordinary yes of an unemotional
     statement, only extended longer. Imagine a
     hero and heroine on the English moors. He asks
     if she will live there with him for the rest of

their days, and she answers clear-eyed and unafraid, Yes. That is the high tone in Chinese, musically expressed.

2. <u>The <u>Rising</u> Tone</u> (<u>Second</u> <u>Tone</u>)
Rises quickly and directly, as in an inquiring yes? What do you want?

3. <u>The <u>Low</u> Tone</u> (<u>Third</u> <u>Tone</u>)
Actually a low, then rising tone. Heard in a doubtful, hesitating yes. It is a dark night and the professor sits alone in his den. He hears his name called outside the heavy wood door. He answers, Yes?

4. <u>The <u>Falling</u> Tone</u> (<u>Fourth</u> <u>Tone</u>)
As in Eisenhower's triumphant Yes!! We've taken Normandy.

Following, an example of one syllable, <u>Ji</u>, in four different tones, written four different ways, having four different meanings:

Jī	High Tone	"property"
Jí	Rising Tone	"anxious"
Jǐ	Low Tone	"annals"
Jì	Falling Tone	"to remember"

Lest the reader think otherwise, the tone is absolutely essential to being understood. Without it, a Chinese will stare at you in polite noncomprehension. Or terrible faux pas can result when tones are confused:

Jū	High Tone	"pig"
Jú	Rising Tone	"bamboo"
Jǔ	Low Tone	"god"
Jù	Falling Tone	"to remember"

Professor Karlgren points out how disastrous it would be for a foreign missionary to confuse ju, "pig" with ju, "god."

The tones are included in the Chinese section of this book for the brave. The Chinese dictionary has the tone number next to the character. The Yale series of books uses the following symbols for the tones when they are used with Chinese words written in English letters, or romanized:

—	╱	⌄	╲
High	Rising	Low	Falling

Ink Stone (Michael McEvoy)

Ink Stick (Laura DeCoppet)

CHAPTER 6

ROMANIZATION

Romanization is a device used to teach Westerners how to pronounce Chinese words. This is simply using alphabet letters to convey the sound of a picture-word. Writing jù for 住 . Picture-language to letter-language. All the words which have been spelled out in this book have been "romanized."

There are two main systems of romanization used in the West at this time: The Yale and the Wade-Giles (from the great sinologists of the same name). The Wade-Giles is the older, and it is a little clumsier, though its approximations of the vowel sounds are excellent. The Yale is streamlined, has less apostrophes and renders the consonants better. Serious students of Chinese must learn both eventually, but beginners learn Yale first. For this reason, Yale is used in this book. Should a person decide to go from this book to a formal study of Chinese, he will already be familiar with the romanization used in the Yale textbooks.

All existing romanizations have a common difficulty: None is completely adequate to represent sounds which do not exist in English.

If you pronounce the romanized words exactly the way they look, more or less, with the help of the pronunciation table from the Yale Dictionary (pp. **x-xvii**), you will be pronouncing Mandarin Chinese. The table will help you to say "fong" when

fang is written, not "fang" as in a snake's tooth. Once you
have the syllable down, put it to tonal music, and sing it out.
Peking Mandarin is slow melodic speech, and if you put sentences
together, using the words in this book, say them as a slow melody.
The sing-song ah-so style is very Hollywood and doesn't have much
to do with actual Chinese.

The question invariably comes up: Wouldn't it be easier
for the Chinese if they just romanized their entire language?
So many more could be literate. The French romanized the
Vietnamese language. Would it work in China?

Professor Karlgren vigorously denies that it would on
several grounds. One, since all dialects pronounce every character
differently, the Peking romanization would make no sense in any
other part of the country, and the script, which makes the written
language intelligible to all dialects, would be lost. Two, the
Chinese would be compelled to discard their 3,000 year old
literation, the backbone of their civilization, since it would
be indecipherable in phonetics, and it would be impossible to
transliterate the whole literature for each dialect separately.
The art of calligraphy would abruptly disappear. What would be
gained is the work of schoolchildren to learn 4,000 characters,
for that is all one needs to learn to be literate.

So, it seems that characters are better left in Chinese,
and romanization is better left to Western students.

CHAPTER 7

THE CHINESE-ENGLISH DICTIONARY

THIS CHAPTER IS INCLUDED FOR STUDENTS WHO MUST (OR
WOULD LIKE TO) CONFRONT AND COME TO TERMS WITH A
CHINESE-ENGLISH DICTIONARY FOR THE FIRST TIME. IF
YOU HAVE NO INTEREST IN SUCH MATTERS, PLEASE SKIP TO
THE NEXT CHAPTER.

Be prepared for an interesting trip. Mathew's Chinese-
English Dictionary is the standard work and has been for some
time. A good Asian library will have a lot of copies. A good
general library should have at least one. If you are studying
Chinese seriously, you should own one. You can order one from
Weiser's, Orientalia, or Paragon, in New York. All three
specialize in Oriental books. (Addresses in back.) Sometimes,
if you are hanging around students, you can pick up a smaller
bootleg edition from Hong Kong. It's cheaper and the size is
better (not so big and heavy).

The first thing you have to get used to is the older
Wade-Giles romanization. If you've been studying formally, you've
probably learned Yale Romanization. But sooner or later you have
to learn Wade-Giles too, so you might as well get the little
pamphlet on it published by Yale. From your school bookstore,
or directly from Far Eastern Publications at Yale. You can
figure out a great deal without any help at all, since it's

mostly common sense anyway.

If you follow the directions in this chapter, and practice a few times, the technique will start to come naturally. It's slow at first, but soon you become a whiz. You won't have to worry about getting practice if you are in a second or third year language class.

At the top of every page, the words are indexed two ways: Alphabetically from A to Ywun, and numerically from 1 to 7773.

TIEN (ㄉㄧㄢ)	6336—6345	(ㄉㄧㄢ) TIEN
HSIANG (ㄒㄧㄤ)	2556—2561	(ㄒㄧㄤ) HSIANG
PING (ㄆㄧㄥ)	5283—5288	(ㄆㄧㄥ) PING

There are two ways to find a word. If you know the pronunciation, you simply look it up the same way you look up a word in an English dictionary, using the alphabetical index. If you don't know how to pronounce it, you look it up by radical, in the radical index, get its number, and look it up by number.

Either way, by number or alphabetically, when you find the character, its meaning appears opposite in bold face, and underneath, expressions and phrases containing it from classical literature and colloquial usage. The small number next to the

鄉[1] The country, as contrasted with the town. A village; a neighbourhood. Distinguish 卿 No. 1155. Anciently a district of 12,500 families; a district of not more than 50,000 inhabitants.
2556

鄉下 the country; one's native place.

鄉下土老 the ignorant country people.

鄉井 one's native place.

鄉人 儺 the villagers drove away the demons of pestilence.

鄉保 or 鄉老 village-elders.

鄉信 (or 書) a letter from home.

鄉俗 local customs.

鄉先生 a country-elder.

鄉先達 a man of one's locality who has made a name for himself.

鄉勇 village-braves.

鄉味 delicacies from one's native place.

鄉君 ancient title given to women.

鄉國 one's native place.

鄉土 or 鄉土科 local geography, productions and history, etc., as a school subject.

鄉士 the criminal officer in charge of six hsiang districts.

鄉廷 depreciatory term used of oneself in addressing seniors from one's district.

鄉官 country gentlemen.

鄉弟 depreciatory term used of oneself in addressing those of the same locality.

鄉愿 a hypocrite; an impostor.

鄉愿德之賊也 you hyper-honest village people are the thieves of virtue.

鄉戶 local people; fellow villagers.

鄉曲 a poor village; my native place.

鄉望 famous in his own district.

鄉末 I—depreciatory term used in speaking of oneself to those of the same place.

鄉村學校 rural district-schools.
鄉村教育 rural education.
鄉村投遞 rural delivery.
鄉村生活 rural life.
鄉民 the people of the villages.
鄉氣 or 鄉風 the customs of a locality; the country air.

鄉乘 villagers; the whole village.

鄉科 or 鄉試 the former triennial examination for the second degree of 舉人.

鄉約 a village-headman appointed by the villagers.

鄉紳 country-gentry.

鄉貢 old name for the former second-degree graduates.

鄉親 fellow-countrymen; of the same village.

鄉評 village-opinions.

鄉豪 village-bullies.

鄉談 or 鄉音 local patois.

鄉貫 or 家鄉 one's native village.

鄉邑報章 provincial newspapers.

鄉鄰 country neighbours.

鄉里 or 鄉村 country villages; one's native place.

鄉長 village-elder.

鄉黨 district-communities.

鄉黨州閭 neighbours.

(a) Read hsiang[4]. u.f., 向 No. 2549. Formerly; towards, etc.

鄉也 just now, a little while ago.

鄉化 to turn towards the right; to reform.

鄉導 to show the way, to guide.

鄉背 front and rear; opposite, contrary.

(b) Conditional particle.

鄉使不守法律 if the laws are not strictly observed.

鄉[4] A little while, formerly. u.f., 向 No. 2549.
2557

鄉役之三月 lately employed him for three months.

鄉者 recently; up till now.

蠁[3,4] Larvae; grubs.
2558

蠁匇 in great haste.

胅蠁 small flies rising in swarms from damp ground—used to illustrate a flourishing state of things.

響[3] Noise, sound, echo. To make a noise.
响
2559
bright.

響亮 a crash; clear-sounding.

響卜 to divine from voices heard on the last evening of the year.

響器 musical instruments.

響尾蛇 the rattlesnake.

響快 prompt, as quick as an echo.

響應 an echo—speedily; to respond.

響箭 sounding-arrow, once used by brigands as a signal.

響聲 a sound; an echo.

響音 noise; sound.

響馬 mounted highwaymen.

饗[3] To offer in sacrifice or at a feast. To enjoy a sacrifice.
2560 —as the gods.

饗祭 or 饗供 to sacrifice.

饗錁 sugar-figures carried at weddings.

上饗 to offer a sacrifice.

尚饗 May this my offering be acceptable to thee—final words of a sacrificial ode.

神饗 offering to the gods.

鄉[4] Opposite; to incline towards. u.f., 向 No. 2549.
嚮
2561

嚮北 facing the north.

嚮午 noon.

嚮往 to desire; to incline to.

嚮慕 to turn towards; to look up to.

嚮 (or 響) 搨 to make a tracing of writings, etc., by holding them up to the light.

嚮明 the hour of dawn.

嚮明而治 matters are best regulated if an early start is made.

嚮晦 the hour of sunset.

嚮晨 the approach of dawn.

嚮背 backwards and forwards contraries.

(a) To guide, to approach.

嚮道 a guide.

嚮邇 to approach; to draw near to.

character tells what tone it is pronounced in.

If you don't know how to pronounce the word, then you need both the meaning and the pronunciation. Using the character 好 , follow these steps:

1. <u>First</u> <u>determine</u> <u>the</u> <u>radical</u> <u>of</u> <u>the</u> <u>character</u>.
   Hint: In a two-part left and right character, the radical is usually the left part.
   In 道 , 辶 is the radical.
   In 洋 , 氵 is the radical.
   At first, you'll probably select on a trial and error basis. Soon you'll know by experience which is the radical. Try the left part, 女 .

2. <u>Next</u> <u>you</u> <u>need</u> <u>the</u> <u>Radical</u> <u>Number</u>.
   Every Mathew's dictionary has a Radical List at the back. The radicals are arranged by number of strokes. Count the number of strokes, go to that section of the list, and find your radical. In the margin you'll find the radical number. Say you want to find the word in the dictionary. You decide 女 is the radical. It has three strokes, so you look in the 3-stroke section, and there it is: The number is 38.

(I deliberately haven't given instructions for stroke counting here because I assume if you're ready to use a Chinese dictionary, you probably know how to count strokes. If you don't see the Chapter on Calligraphy, p. 74.)

THE 214 RADICALS.

N.B.—The numbers in the Dictionary under which the Radicals occur may be ascertained from the Radical Index. The more common Radicals are printed in large type. Such abbreviated forms as, e. g., Nos. 9, 18, etc., do not usually stand alone, but are found in combination only.

Strokes					
1 一	23 匸	46 山	68 斗	92 牙	115 禾
1 一	24 十	47 巛 川 巜	69 斤	93 牛 牛	116 穴
2 ｜	25 卜	48 工	70 方	94 犬 犭	117 立
3 丶	26 卩	49 己	71 无 旡	**5**	**6**
4 丿	27 厂	50 巾	72 日	95 玄	118 竹 ⺮
5 乙	28 厶	51 干	73 曰 日	96 玉 王 王	119 米
6 亅	29 又	52 幺	74 月	97 瓜	120 糸 糸
2	**3**	53 广	75 木	98 瓦	121 缶
7 二	30 口	54 廴	76 欠	99 甘	122 网 罒 ⺲
8 亠	31 囗	55 廾	77 止	100 生	123 羊
9 人 亻	32 土	56 弋	78 歹	101 用	124 羽
10 儿	33 士	57 弓	79 殳	102 田	125 老 而
11 入	34 夂	58 彑 彐	80 毋	103 疋	126 而
12 八	35 夊	59 彡	81 比	104 疒	127 耒
13 冂	36 夕	60 彳	82 毛	105 癶	128 耳
14 冖	37 大	**4**	83 氏	106 白	129 聿
15 冫	38 女	61 心 忄 忄	84 气	107 皮	130 肉 月
16 几	39 子	62 戈	85 水 氵	108 皿	131 臣
17 凵	40 宀	63 戶	86 火 灬	109 目 罒	132 自
18 刀 刂	41 寸	64 手 扌	87 爪 爫	110 矛	133 至
19 力	42 小 尣	65 支	88 父	111 矢	134 臼
20 勹	43 尢 尢	66 攴 攵	89 爻	112 石	135 舌
21 匕	44 尸	67 文	90 爿	113 示 礻	136 舛
22 匚	45 屮		91 片	114 禸	137 舟

If you are serious about learning Chinese, some day you will probably memorize all the radicals and their numbers. This is not as difficult as it sounds, since using them over and over again is enough to commit many of them to memory. When you know the radical numbers by heart, you can eliminate this step completely.

3. <u>Go to the Radical Index and use the Radical Number to locate your character</u>.

The Radical Index is also in the back of Mathew's. It is divided into 214 sections, one for each radical. Every character having 女 as a radical appears in the 女 section. This is where you find your word number.

In the 女 section, the characters are grouped by number of strokes <u>besides the radical</u>. First the words having one additional stroke, then the words having two additional strokes, and so on.

Since 女 is the radical, then 好 (plus three additional strokes), it will be located under the heading of Radical 38, in the section of three stroke words. The number of your word will be in the margin. Get it. That's what you're after. It is 2062.

堤 6231	城 576	壞 3784	壬 3100	夗 7713	奇 511	爽 5327	妝 1151	妒 3422
壥 6317	壐 454	壆 2779	壮 1453	夙 5502	奄 7378	奮 1874		姻 7408
塤 3254	塲 218	壄 3337	壳 3406	多 6416	奈 4615		5	娃 6990
塔 625	塴 4331	壁 5113	声 5748	夜 7315		↓	姐 766	姱 3528
堭 3295	堛 1023	壈 5537	垂 1478	夠 3419	6	38	姊 6948	姦 817
堵 6497	境 1136	塞 7555	壺 2187		奐 2248		姒 5594	姨 2985
	墓 4586		壻 2836	夢 4433	奕 3022	女 4776	姍 5416	姸 7340
10	墖 1067	14	壹 3016	夤 2397	契 551		妻 555	娍 5560
塚 1516	壄 926	壓 7231	壺 3687	夥 7427	奔 5028	2	姑 3453	姝 7051
堨 2908	聖 5876	壔 2128	壽 5846		奎 3643	奶 4613	姰 2829	娸 5850
塘 6117	廪 328	壔 6127		37	夋 74	奴 4753	始 5772	娈 6924
寨 5446		壏 2908	34	大 5943	夌 6808	↓	姊 4613	姜 637
塍 387	12	壐 2469	夂 962			3	妮 4657	姥 4583
垠 6572	壥 5647	壤 2068		1	7	她 5961	妹 4410	娃 992
墊 6525	境 738		1	夫 1908	奎 6160	妄 7035	妹 4547	
塗 7466	塼 6886	15	夆 654	夬 3535	奕 2425	妁 5830	姉 6948	7
堝 7168	墩 669	壜 3605	备 1877	天 6361	奘 6700	如 3137	姐 5946	娩 7012
塤 6373	墝 6572	壘 4228		太 6020		妾 704	姆 4583	娛 7647
壤 5492	增 6763		35	夭 7277	8	妍 2062	姓 2770	娓 7110
塑	墦 1791	16	夊 5517		臬 53	妃 1838	姗 1377	娣 6202
塪 7148	墣 2823	壌 6069		2	奄 3643	奸 818	姑 6503	媤 433
塌 5967	墢 6069	壚 4157	夌 1736	失 5806			委 7098	娥 4781
塔 5978	墥 1868	壞 2232	复 1991	央 7239	9	4	姜 814	娑 5455
壡 6702	境 6566	遺 7117	夏 2521		奢 5696	妞 4738		娟 1628
塊 3550	墜 1471	壐 4261	夐 2816	3—4	奠 6357	妌 7602	6	娉 5312
	墮 6427			夸 3526		姶 1054	姮 2106a	娘 4683
11	墨 4386	17—21	3—4	夷 2982	10—11	妊 3102	姣 704	娠 312
墈 3255		壤 3078	夒 3662	夾 611	奥 46	妖 7279	姓 3102	娌 4745
墊 6359	13	壥 4843			奋 3997	妙 4474	姚 5720	娜 3860
壞 4140	壇 6059		36	5	奪 6433	妒 6503	姬 7269	
墊 5894	墙 674	33	夕 2485		奬 657	妓 439	姫 408	8
壙 7578	壚 387	士 5776	外 7001	奉 1884	奭 5102	妨 1804	姞 3624	娼 7227
						妣 5082	姞 477	
						安 6454		

32 土
33 士
34 夂
35 夊
36 夕
37 大
38 女

4.   Take the number and find your word. Use the
     numerical index at the page tops. Make a note
     of the word number, pronunciation, tone, and
     meaning. It will save you some work.

NOTE: If your character doesn't appear in the Radical
Index under the radical you've selected, you've chosen
the wrong radical. It happens. Try again. If none
of the radicals you choose is right (it happens), you've
got a tricky character. It will be found by number
of strokes in the handy list which also appears at the
back of Mathew's: Characters Having Obscure Radicals.

If you find the instructions confusing, try them actually
holding a dictionary in your hands and locating a few characters
step by step. Try the character 德 as in 道德經 Dau De Ching.
If you decide 彳 is the radical (being the left part), look in
the List of Radicals under 3 strokes. There it is, Radical 60.
Now, to the Radical Index, Radical 60 Section. There it is.
Now, you have 12 additional strokes, so you find the 12-stroke
section. Lo! The character is here, and beside it, the number
you've been looking for, 6162. Turn to the page having this
number indexed at the top (page 889), find the word. It pronounces
De, and means virtue.

Those of little faith will never believe such a system
works, but it does, and two or three days at it will make you a
champion.

HINT: If you have a long passage or selection to translate, with a lot of words you don't know, comb it, picking out all the words and listing them in a column. Then using the radical index, get the numbers for all the words, and write them down next to the characters. Then go down the list of numbers, and write the meaning next to the character. Now start to translate the text referring to the word list whenever necessary. This saves more time than doing all the steps for each word as you go along, and you can concentrate on translating better. If you are translating a particular text, keep a notebook and all your word lists will be together when you have an exam.

> The fundamental inspiration of calligraphy
> as of all the arts in China is Nature.
>
> Chiang Yee, *Chinese Calligraphy*.

Chinese script, a genuine product of the creative power
of the Chinese mind, and not, like our writing, a loan
from unrelated peoples, distant in time and space, is
cherished and revered in China to a degree that we can
hardly understand. And this regard is the greater
because its picturesque and varying form appeals to the
imagination infinitely more than our jejune and matter-
of-fact script. . . . The Chinese script has always been
extensively drawn upon for artistic purposes. Calligraphy
is the mother of Chinese pictorial art and always its
intimate ally, and an expert calligrapher has always been
just as much esteemed in China as a painter of the first
rank.

Professor Bernhard Karlgren, *Sound and Symbol in Chinese*,
52.

CHAPTER 8

CALLIGRAPHY

Calligraphy, art of beautiful writing, is the most popular art in China. The visual nature of the Chinese script is partly responsible. It is a national taste, a common aesthetic instinct nourished from childhood up. Painting, calligraphy and literature are intertwined in China. A painter will add a poem to his painting, something he composed, or something from classical literature. He displays his prowess at calligraphy in the composition. The Chinese consider beautiful writing enhances the painting. Some calligraphers will paint characters on a rock overlooking a particularly beautiful scene--the poem selected will be apropos, and the handwriting will magnify nature. If a famous art collector, say an emperor, has a fine hand, he will, perhaps, add a line or two of his own to a painting. Far from ruining the painting, this increases its value. Together, poetry, calligraphy, and painting create a total effect. "Calligraphy, we might say, is the main stem of Chinese graphic symbolism. Painting is its deciduous foliage." (Willett, p. 308.) Calligraphy is a part of life, of street life and home life in China.

Children must learn a good hand as soon as they enter school. They write 10 medium-sized characters a day, adding twenty small ones when they are older. Every Chinese house will have an example of fine handwriting hung as we would hang a painting. Even the poorest family will own a rubbing of calligraphy from an ancient bronze or a stone carving.

The streets, shops and markets of China are strewn with calligraphy--there is not so much reliance on the printed word, there is not the availability of technology which produces printed words. The Chinese consider the printed word "dead" in appearance and inferior to the written word. They respect the written word so much that they are taught never to tear up or throw away a sheet of paper with writing--it is taken to a special temple and burned.

The thousands of _literati_, the powerful class which ran the government of China, from the national down to the town level, were, all of them, calligraphers. In point of fact, a good hand was indispensable for entrance to the civil service of China.

Calligraphy is a highly refined art but its roots are in the earth. Hundreds of books have been written by calligraphers analyzing, categorizing and synthesizing it, but "the fundamental inspiration of calligraphy, as of all the arts in China, is nature" (Chiang Yee, p. 111). The writing must be alive and moving. A static perfectly symmetrical motionless design does not appeal to Chinese taste, while "dynamic asymmetry" does.

Just as Professor Karlgren must finally use the imagery of architecture to finally describe Chinese characters, so Professor Yee says that calligraphy, like the dance, has "impulse, momentum, momentary poise, and the interplay of active force." (p. 117) Nothing in nature is regular, so the well-written character, following nature, is irregular in some way. (pp. 123-124)

> During the long course of our artistic
> history, innumerable writers have made
> exhaustive researches into the possible
> variations of stroke and structural form,
> with the result that there is now hardly
> an organic shape or a movement of a living
> thing that has not been assimilated into
> our calligraphy. The great masters of the
> past set themselves to absorb natural
> beauties and to translate them into the
> strokes and structures of characters, and
> their successors have classified their
> achievements. . . .
>
> You will find examples of strokes inspired
> by the brittleness of the sheep's leg, by
> the massive paw of the tiger, the rugged
> face of a rock, the heavy tread of the
> elephant, the twisted shape of the pine
> branch, the firmness and straightness of
> the chestnut trunk, the elegance of the
> orchid leaves . . . the creeping movement
> of the snake. (113-114)

The line is the medium of all the graphic arts. Alphabets

are limited to curves and straight lines in their construction.

Chinese calligraphy alone explores and celebrates the abstract

beauty of the line.

The character is made up of brush strokes. Once the eye

becomes accustomed to seeing these seemingly random arrangements

of lines as part of a logical whole, the business of approaching

the Chinese language becomes much less forbidding. The basic

pictures (the 214 radicals) become familiar with a little use,

as does the general style of representation. Once the pictures

were very literal representations, and so closely corresponded

to nature that they were more readily recognized. This can be

64

seen in the old versions of characters given in the Chinese
section of this book.

Brush strokes are different kinds and shapes of lines used
to write characters. To begin to write characters well, one
must learn the varieties of line, the brush strokes. There are
seven basic strokes. There is a definite technique for the
writing of each stroke, with variations of turn and pressure
used to achieve the different angles, curves, widths, bumps and
points. The calligrapher desires the ideal, and the concentration
required to produce it brings a relaxed, lucid, peaceful state
of mind. If the would-be calligrapher can perfect each stroke
in its ideal form, he is assured a finer hand when he puts them
together to form characters. Calligraphy is an aid to remembering
characters, for in order to write a character, you must pay
attention to all its details, especially the groupings of pictures
which form it. Thus it becomes an orderly composition to the eye,
rather than a haphazard squiggly chaos.

DIRECTIONS FOR THE SEVEN BASIC STROKES   (FROM CHIANG YEE.)

1.   HORIZONTAL STROKES   (Heng)

Written to seem like a formation of cloud stretching
from a thousand miles away and abruptly terminating.

<u>Direction</u> <u>of</u> <u>brush</u>: To make this stroke, the brush moves slightly to the left, then to the right for the main length of the stroke, then turns slightly left to lift off the paper.

<u>Pressure</u> <u>of</u> <u>the</u> <u>Brush</u>: Greater pressure at the beginning, to produce the "bone" effect (<u>tun</u>, 70% of the length of the hair touching the paper). Raise the brush slightly in the middle (<u>ti</u>, 50% of the length of the hairs touching the paper), greater pressure at the end.

2.   <u>DOTS</u> (Dyan)

The impression of a rock falling with all its force from a high cliff.

<u>Direction</u> <u>and</u> <u>Pressure</u>: All dots begin with the pressure slight, then increase. When the main movement of any stroke is to the left, one begins writing to the right slightly with very little pressure. This is to get the brush on the page, and to build up momentum for the main left movement of the stroke. The initial right movement will not be visible, since the brush passes over it when it travels left again. At the end of the stroke, the brush turns

back to the right slightly. This finishes the
stroke, and will not leave a visible trail when you
try to lift the brush off the page, thus ruining
the character.

3. SWEEPING LEFT STROKES   (Pye)

Sweep downward, written from right to left. Having
sharp sword edges or resembling gleaming rhinoceros
horns.

Direction and Pressure: Begin by travelling upward
slightly, then downward to the point. The tun (70%)
pressure at the beginning, then decreasing pressure to
the end. Pressure is decreased by lifting hand and
brush straight up from the wrist until it is not
touching the page. Pressure is increased by vertically
bearing down.

4. VERTICAL STROKES   (Chih)

Like a thousand year old vine stem, still stout
and strong.

Direction and Pressure: All begin with a slight
upward movement, then downward. The first, taper to
a point by slowly lifting the brush straight off the

page. The second, turns upward and to the left
slightly. The third, turns upward and to the left more.

5.   <u>HOOKS</u>, <u>SHARP</u> <u>CURVES</u>   (Wan)

Like the sinews and joints of a strong crossbow,
pliable, but tough.

<u>Direction</u> <u>and</u> <u>Pressure</u>: The first is a hook named
after a bow. Start the brush by moving slightly
upward, then horizontal, then turn downward for the
hook, swinging upward slightly at the end for the
point. To make the horizontal hook, the brush moves
from the left, inclining to the right until the line
becomes horizontal, then finishes by curving up the
left for the point.

6.   <u>SWEEPING</u> <u>RIGHT</u> <u>STROKES</u>   (Na)

These are made from left to right like a wave
suddenly rolling up.

<u>Direction</u> <u>and</u> <u>Pressure</u>: This starts with a slight
movement to the left, then sweeps right, the <u>tun</u>
(70%) pressure is used at the end toward the right to
gain the flat level shape.

7. <u>DOWNWARD</u> <u>STROKE</u>

Straighter and stiffer than Na. Appearing like a
dropping pine tree with firm roots.

Practice these strokes repeatedly until you can produce the
desired shape, and your control of the brush is good. Once you
master each of the strokes, and have a familiar and fond feeling
for it, your characters will become more shapely and beautiful.

<u>The</u> <u>correct</u> <u>position</u> <u>of</u> <u>the</u> <u>brush</u>.
Here are some technical instructions, with apologies for
the deadly prose it produces. The brush is held <u>vertically</u>. The
thumb and three fingers when placed properly support the brush
vertically with no effort. The thumb is on the left side of the
handle. The second finger is on the right side about an inch
above the thumb, the handle resting against it. The third
finger is slightly below the thumb curving over the front of the
brush. The fourth finger touches the brush at the base of the
fingernail.

The thumb and second finger give the main energy, direction
and pressure. The third and fourth turn and move the brush.
The pinky, held behind the fourth, supports the hand, gives
added firmness, and assists in direction. All five fingers play
an important part.

The strength of the wrist should flow into the brush, then
into the stroke. The brush should be held firmly. A favorite

DOTS:

PYE:

JR:

HOOKS:

NA:

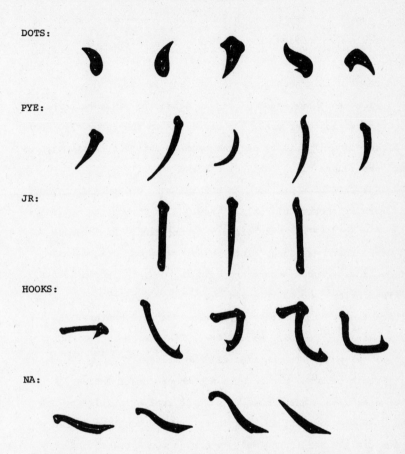

The examples appearing on Pp. 64-69 are reproduced by permission of the author and publishers from CHINESE CALLI-GRAPHY: AN INTRODUCTION TO ITS AESTHETIC AND TECHNIQUE, 3rd Edition, Revised and Enlarged, by Chiang Yee, Copyright 1973 by the President and Fellows of Harvard College.

trick of Chinese calligraphy masters was to sneak up behind their pupils and try to snatch the brush from their hands. If they could not succeed, the pupil showed promise. "A very tight hold produces rugged, severe, powerful strokes; a rather looser hold results in graceful, tender and supple ones."

Width and narrowness of stroke depend on pressure. The whole brush is never used, but serves as an ink reservoir. For a narrow line (Ti, to raise) the hand is raised so that only half the length of the hairs touch the paper.

For the thick part of the stroke, more pressure is needed, and more of the brush (70%) is used. (See Chiang Yee, p. 145.)

Each stroke has many different varieties. For example, of hooks there are long, flat, phoenix-wing and dragon-tail. Of vertical strokes, there are dropping dew, suspended needle, perpendicular, and sheep's leg.

A famous calligrapher says, when you have mastered the seven strokes, you will be able to write the character "hung" (eternity) well. It contains all the strokes.

It is obvious, since there are thousands of Chinese characters, that there must be some general principles to be followed when writing any character. They cannot be formed haphazardly. First, one must determine the "stroke" order. Second, one must plan the composition of the character.

<u>The</u> <u>general</u> <u>principles</u> <u>of</u> <u>stroke</u> <u>order</u> <u>are</u>:

1. Begin at the upper left-hand corner, proceed to
    the lower right-hand corner.

2. Begin at the left, proceed to the right.

3. Begin at the top, proceed to the bottom.

4. Begin with the outside, proceed to the inside.

5. Begin with horizontal lines, then do the lines
    crossing the horizontal.

6. Do slanting left stroke first, then slanting right stroke.

7. Do center stroke before symmetrical wings.

(Using this method, it is easy to count the strokes in a
character in order to find it in a dictionary.)

It is not enough just to select a spot on a sheet of paper and fill it up with a character. One must attend to every detail: the relation of the part to the whole, the length of a stroke in relation to the others, the width at different parts of each stroke, and in relation to each other. Angles must be well-defined, not written as curves; the correct degree of slant or tilt must be given to each part. The center of gravity must fall upon the base so the character has a stable stance. (CY, 117.) The entire character must possess strength. The lines must balance the spaces.

An anonymous writer of the Tang Dynasty invented a device to use in plotting the parts in relation to the whole. This is the nine-fold square.

(From a "How-to" Booklet on Calligraphy published in Hong Kong.)

It provides a grid to estimate balance, mass and space. The character should not be too crowded or too "loose." It should not be dense on one side, thin on the other. A vertical stroke should pinion the character it passes through as in 中 (see p. 125). Characters which are "face to face" should not be too far apart (p. 179); those "back to back" should not be too close, as in (p. 124). The roof radical (p. 165) must well cover the sections which come under it. Parts which fill a square (p. 162) must not leave large spaces nor fill the square to bursting. A narrow vertical stroke must appear as a stake in the ground. Characters with two or three parts of equal value should have the effect of people of equal rank meeting one another. A curved stroke or hook which encircles other elements must have the effect of wrapping it up and embracing it (p. 202).

The grid of squares can be used to adjust the weight of the shapes against each other and to judge the balance between the spaces and the masses. As to balance, Chiang Yee says: "The balance is achieved by instinct and derives from the writer's aesthetic vision."

Finally, no stroke must ever be corrected, since "touching up" destroys the life-force of the stroke. It must stay as it comes from the brush, or the entire stroke must be repeated.

For practicing, a good method is to outline a nine-fold square on a piece of graph paper with a black felt-tip pen. Place this under the sheet of rice paper as a guide while you plan the composition. Practice a single character repeatedly until you are pleased that you have captured it. Then leave that character for the day, moving on to another until you succeed at that one. Keep the ones you like for future comparison. If you are seriously interested, find a calligraphy instructor and take lessons.

<u>MATERIALS</u>:

One of the nicest things about calligraphy is the materials. These, called the "Four Precious Things of the Scholar's Table," are: inkstone, inkstick, brush and paper. Throughout Chinese history, fine examples of each of these have been highly prized by scholars, and have been "cult-objects" of the ancient ritual of calligraphy.

The inkstone, used for grinding ink, has an all-over rectangular shape. At one end there is a flat high place where the grinding is done, then an incline, then a well where the ink collects.

Inkstones have been made of stone, iron, copper, pottery, glass, oyster-shell, bamboo, wood, jade, even gold and silver. If a teacher or a friend made a present of one, it was highly valued, especially if it belonged to a famous person. One famous scholar possessed one formed naturally by rain and frost. He called it "Ink Mountain," and compared it to a miniature world with peaks, terraces, and mountains.

The inkstick, durable and economic, has been the most popular form of commercial ink for 1,000 years in China. No inkstick is considered mature until it is at least a few years old. Chinese collectors hoard old inksticks. Ancient sticks of certain famous makers commanded fantastic prices. Some reputedly became worth their weight in gold.

A story has it that a certain scholar of the Sung Dynasty owned an inkstick made by one Li Ting-Gwei. It was thin as a chopstick and less than a foot long. He and his brother used it for over ten years writing at the rate of some 500 characters a day! (Willett, 294.)

The inkstick is ground with water to make fresh ink every time one writes. It is in the shape of a long rectangle with a gold design and calligraphy on it. It is dipped into a porcelain bowl of water and rubbed back and forth to make ink. Rub until you attain the desired consistency and blackness. It is wise to make enough to last your entire session, if you are working on a scroll which will contain a number of characters, since the inks from two or more batches will not be the same color. If you are lazy and do not want to grind your own ink, it is now possible to buy sumi-ink in art supply stores or in Japanese stores in liquid form. Thus, for practicing, everything will come out the same color, and you will not waste the excess which is sometimes left over when grinding. But bear in mind, please, that this is a highly unorthodox procedure. You should always keep several saucer-size white porcelain plates. These can be used to take the ink down to lighter or thinner blacks. Just dip the inked brush into water and blend a lighter black on the porcelain dish.

Inkstones and inksticks are now mass-produced and can be bought very cheaply in boxed sets with two or three brushes, or separately. Look for them in art supply stores or Japanese stores. They are sometimes called sumi-sets, from the Japanese painting.

Chinese writing is now commonly done on rice paper, but formerly, as early as three centuries before Christ, silk was the material in use everywhere. Paper came into use in Han times, 600 years before the Arabs used it and 1,000 years before the Europeans. Chinese tradition states that in 105 A.D. an Officer of the Imperial Guard suggested it to the Emperor as a cheap substitute for silk. It completely replaced silk within a generation.

Rice paper is translucent and more absorbent than the papers Westerners normally use. Rice paper "takes" the ink into its fibers because it has a coarser texture and slight nap. It can be bought in sheets or rolls of varying quality, also in art supply and Japanese stores.

There are many specimens of fine Chinese papers from the 1st to 10th centuries still surviving. By the Sung Dynasty, the scholar could buy papers with fancy brand names and trademarks. Just as the best inksticks were hoarded, so the best papers were saved for use long after they were made. The most famous paper ever made was from young bamboo pulp for the last ruler of the Southern Tang (959-975). By the 11th century it was rare, and the competition among calligraphers and painters for even a small piece was fierce. A Western observer, on seeing this paper at a London exhibition in 1935 commented: "The paper was covered with a barely visible embossed pattern of lotuses. Another had an all-over design of melon vines." (Willett, 295.)

As for the Chinese brush, it has a hollow bamboo handle, and finely pointed animal-hair tip. It comes stiff-pointed with some sort of sizing, and the entire point should not be broken in, only the tip. Never select a brush with stray or broken hairs, since they will leave little lines of ink, thus spoiling your characters. They come in about ten sizes, though only three perhaps, will be needed to begin with--two medium-sized and a small.

The brush is a much more flexible writing instrument than a pen. Formerly, painters and calligraphers made their own. A great variety of hair has been used in the past, different periods having their preferences. Rabbit was the most popular in the Han. The Tang painter, Ou-Yang Tung favored a core of fox fringed with rabbit. Another Tang painter liked a stiff brush (made of fox and deer) called "Hen's Claws." During the Five Dynasties, a Mongol painter used wolf hair--an apt material for a former nomadic tribesman. Two famous Sung painters used a brush produced by a Szchwan family of brushmakers, made from mouse whisker fringed with sheep's wool. Other Sung painters like brushes made from the hair of human children. Today painters favor rabbit for more delicate work, sheep and goat for bold work, and for the rest choose between sable, wolf, fox, deer, hare and hog-bristle. (Willett, 293.)

Chinese calligraphy is a huge subject. Those interested in further information, especially for samples of the many different styles, should see Chiang Yee's excellent work, Chinese Calligraphy. It is hoped that the reader will try his hand.

Extensive knowledge of Chinese is not necessary, for as
Professor Yee says:

> "Every Chinese character presents to the
> calligrapher an almost infinite variety
> of problems of structure and composition;
> and when executed it presents to the reader
> a formal design the abstract beauty of
> which is capable of drawing the mind away
> from the literal meaning of the characters.
> Many of our scholars have confessed that
> they have almost lost their minds contemplat-
> ing the miraculous lines and structures of
> some of our characters--characters so
> combined as to introduce to the thought
> aesthetically satisfying equilibria of visual
> forces and movements. For there is in every
> piece of fine Chinese writing a harmony which
> is a source of pleasure over and above the
> pleasure of apprehending the thought."
> (<u>Chinese</u> <u>Calligraphy</u>, 107.)

CHAPTER 9

GRAMMAR

There is a beautiful story about an extremely precocious little boy in the science-fiction novel <u>Odd</u> <u>John</u> by Olaf Stapledon. He set about learning language by reading the grammar books three or four times, and memorizing lists of words used in common speech, then he began to use the language. The attitude is splendid, though in life the process may take a little longer. This book is intended to be a tool for that type of undertaking. Contrary to popular legend, Chinese is not the most difficult language in the world. For us, it is simply the most inaccessible. But it is masterable, and the key, of course, is in the grammar.

Grammar, since the days it usually issued from antique latinized texts and antique latinized teachers, has had a worse reputation than devils and junkies. Chinese grammar is a whiz. It is very different from English grammar, because English is what the linguists call an inflected language. What this means is that the way English shows how a word is functioning, the way English expresses grammatical relationships is: by varying the endings of words.

Pronouns, for instance. He, his, him. Subject, possessive, object. Depending on how you use the word, you have to vary the form. HE reads. It is HIS book. She told HIM. Latin nouns have ten forms, five cases, singular and plural, and in this respect is the mother of them all. Verbs, for instance: Study, studied, studying. Present, past, progressive. You have to vary the form of the verb for number, time (tense), whether the action flows into the object or back to the subject (voice), and whether the mood is indicative, subjunctive or imperative.

This does not happen at all in Chinese. There are no forms to learn (only characters). Verbs are not conjugated. Nouns are not declined. Wherever a character appears, however it is used, it appears the same way, without variation . . .

For instance, noun as subject:

他念書. Tā nyán-shū.　　He is studying.

Noun as indirect object:

給他錢. Gěi tā chyán.　　Give him money.

Or to quote Professor Karlgren at length:

> Chinese to a very large extent does without formal marks indicating "parts of speech." An object, a 'thing,' concrete or abstract, such as 'man' or 'delight,' is such that it can be the subject of a predicate, or the object of an action, or it can appear as a possessor . . . The Indo-European languages denote these functions by means of various affixes, and the different forms so used make up what are termed paradigms, e. g. the Latin paradigm homo, hominem, hominis, homines, hominum, etc. constituting the grammatical category 'noun.' Latin thus has a formal word-class 'noun' corresponding to the psychological category 'thing.' Similarly a formal category 'verb' is created, answering essentially to the psychological category 'action, process' in paradigms such as the English call, calls, called, where the endings -s and -ed indicate typical aspects of the process. The Chinese have of course the same categories as we have, but it it only to a small extent that they employ form elements defining a word as belonging to a definite 'part-of-speech'; mostly the Chinese syllable is identical whether it is a noun or a verb. (SSC, 56.)

Chinese does have a few ways of indicating form, very few. They are used for clarity and are not obligatory. One way is auxiliaries. For example, yau 要 , in the colloquial speech, when used alone means to want, but when it is used before another verb, it indicates the future tense.

我要書.　　Wǒ yàu shū.　　I want a book.

我要來.　　Wǒ yàu lái.　　I will come.

Another such word is le 了 , which indicates completed action when it follows a verb.

你來了.　　Nǐ lái-le.　　You came.

Still another example is de 的 , which follows a word or word-group and indicates the word-group modifies whatever noun follows.

他買的書好.　　Tā màide shū hǎu.　　The book which he bought is good.

These three, which do indicate form, are the main exceptions which the reader will have to bear in mind. They are explained more fully later on in this chapter, and again in the Chinese section.

If Chinese words are fluid and do not belong to rigidly fixed parts-of-speech, how can Chinese make sense?

A FIXED UNAMBIGUOUS WORD-ORDER

Everything in a logical, proper, ingeniously natural place. Very natural to English-speaking people. Subject-verb-object . . . Modifiers before nouns, not after, as in French and Spanish. English-speaking people learn the sentence patterns. Since the word order never varies, once the pattern is memorized, it can be used for any sentence.

Rather than discourse here in the abstract, this book will first give the categories of words which occur in Chinese and tell the difference between them. Then the book gives basic sentence patterns.

And this is how the reader will learn Chinese. A fixed unambiguous word-order means the sequence is always the same. There is a place for everything, and it is all quite logical. Once you understand the pattern and commit it to memory, you simply use the words you need to express your meaning.

THE CHINESE PARTS OF SPEECH

All Chinese parts of speech are used exclusively with nouns or exclusively with verbs. This distinction kept in mind, there should be no confusion.

NOUNS: Exactly like English nouns. Chinese nouns are the names of persons, places, animals or things.

VERBS: The verb is the most distinctive part of speech in Chinese. Though there are several different types, all verbs are verbs because they can take a negative prefix. Definition: a word that can be negated is a verb.

是 shr̀, "to be"

我是	Wǒ shr̀.	I am.
你是	Nǐ shr̀.	You are.
他是	Tā shr̀.	He/she is.
我們是	Wǒmen shr̀.	We are.
你們是	Nǐmen shr̀.	You are.
他們是	Tāmen shr̀.	They are.

Chinese verbs do not change endings as English verbs do. The same form is used for all persons and numbers.

The Stative Verb expresses a quality or condition. It is used for descriptive statements, there is no action involved. The English equivalent is:

> TO BE + ADJECTIVE

as in to be pretty, 好看 hǎukàn. In Chinese, the to be is included in the character. Definition: A word that can be preceded by the adverb very, 很 hen, is a stative verb.

好	hǎu	to be good
很好	hén hǎu	to be very good
高	gāu	to be tall
很高	hén gāu	to be very tall

The stative verb may stand as a complete verb. It may have adverbs as modifiers. Or it may serve as an ADJECTIVE, and modify nouns. A prime example of the Chinese part-of-speech being fluid. The abbreviation for stative verb in the pattern section is SV.

The Action Verb: This verb is exactly like English verbs which express action or occurence. They may stand alone or may take objects, direct and indirect. They are abbreviated V. (The Yale books call these Functive Verbs.)

Auxiliary Verbs: A special use of an ordinary verb. Abbreviation AV. It precedes another verb and furthers its meaning, the same as English. The pattern is: N AV V .

我們要吃飯. Wǒmen yàu chrfàn. We want to eat.
你得去. Nǐ děi chyù. You must go.

<u>Equative</u> <u>Verbs</u> are used to connect two nouns. The most common one is 是 shŕ, <u>to be</u>.

我是女人.	Wǒ shŕ nyǔ-rén.	I am a woman.
孔子是中國人.	Kǔng-dz shŕ jūng-gwo rén.	Confucius was a Chinese.

<u>Verb-Object</u>: The verb-object compound consists of a verb and the general object logically implied. The two have such a close relationship that they translate as one word (the object is not translated). To translate literally would be redundant. If a specific object is mentioned, it replaces the general object. The abbreviation: VO.

<u>VO</u>	Romanization	Literal Translation	Normal Translation
吃飯	chrfàn	eat-food	eat
説話	shwōhwà	speak-words	talk
唱歌兒	chānggēr	sing-song	sing

<u>ADJECTIVE</u>: These are stative verbs which modify nouns. Sometimes an adjective or group of words modifying a noun will be followed by the word 的 de. This word is simply a grammatical indicator (particle) with no inherent meaning of its own. It says, the modifier is ending.

很高的男人.	hěn gāude nánrén.	The very tall man.
他們寫的書.	Tāmen syède shū.	The book which they wrote.

(If a simple sentence modifies a noun, you can supply a <u>which</u> or <u>who</u> in English as in the second sentence above.)

The pattern for adjectives is: <u>Adj N</u> or <u>Adj de N</u>
or <u>N V de N</u>.

<u>SPECIFIERS</u>: The specifier points to a definite thing.
It modifies nouns and is exactly like the English demonstrative
pronouns <u>this</u> and <u>that</u>. Sometimes they are translated <u>the</u>,
a definite article, since Chinese doesn't have articles.
Abbreviation: SP. The most important specifiers:

這	jèi	this
那	nèi	that
哪	něi	which

Specifiers cannot stand alone, but must always be used
with a measure.

<u>THE</u> <u>MEASURE</u> indicates a unit of measurement or classifica-
tion of a noun. We have measures in English, but they are only
used with certain nouns: a <u>glass</u> of wine, a <u>herd</u> of elephants,
a <u>sheet</u> of paper, a <u>sheaf</u> of wheat, a <u>rasher</u> of bacon. <u>EVERY</u>
Chinese noun must be preceded by a measure when referred to
specifically (as in <u>this</u> book, <u>that</u> pen) or in definite amounts
(<u>three</u> tables, <u>four</u> chairs).

A general measure which may be used for all nouns is 個 <u>ge</u>.
Most nouns have a measure which classifies them with other nouns
which share a common trait. This special measure is preferred
to <u>ge</u>, but in a pinch if you don't remember the special measure,
use <u>ge</u>. It's simply not as elegant, but you will be understood.
張 <u>jāng</u> is used for paper, paintings, tables, and other square
sheet-like things. 本 <u>běn</u> is used for books. 位 <u>wèi</u> is a
term of respect for people. The measure isn't translated into

English unless there is an equivalent expression. But going
from English to Chinese, you must include the measure even though
it is not expressed in English. A book is yi-ben-shu, three
paintings is san-jang-hwar.

There is a reason why the measure developed in the colloquial speech. Just as tones helped distinguish between words
pronounced exactly alike when there were too many of these
words for intelligibility, the measure was for differentiation.

The measure distinguished between nouns which might
otherwise sound the same. The syllable shan means mountain,
and it also means shirt. Thus yi-shan can mean one shirt and
also one mountain. Enter the measure to straighten this out.
Dzwo is used for sites, and chwan is used for articles of clothing.
So, i-dzwo-shan is one (site of) mountain and yi-chwan-shan is
one (article of) shirt. The measure is abbreviated M.

The pattern for Specifiers and Measures is: SP M N.
It translates "this ____" or "that ____" or "which ____?"

這個人	jèige rén	this man
這本書	jèibèn shū	this book
這張畫兒	jèijāng hwār	this painting
那個人	nèige rén	that man
那本書	nèibèn shū	that book
那張畫兒	nèijāng hwār	that painting

Or, the specifier-measure may stand alone as a pronoun.

這個好，那個不好.   Jèige hǎu, nèige bùhǎu.
                     This is good, that isn't.

When referring to a definite amount of things (such as three books or four people), use the pattern: Number M N.

三本書　　　　sān-běn shū　　　three books
四張畫兒　　　sz̀-jāng hwār　　four paintings

When referring to a particular group of things, use the pattern: Sp Nu M N.

這三本書　　　jèi sānběn shū　　these three books
那四張畫兒　　nèi sz̀jāng hwār　those four paintings

The patterns then are: Sp M N, Nu M N, and Sp Nu M N.

NUMBERS are used with nouns for counting, enumerating things, and measuring. There are two types of numbers: pure numbers and numbers with measures. Pure numbers are used for pure counting, years, mathematics and telephone numbers. Numbers with measures indicate the quantity of things when objects are counted.

	Pure Numbers	
一	yī	one
二	èr	two
三	sān	three
四	sz̀	four
	Number-Measure	
一個	yíge	one (thing)
兩個	lyǎngge	two (things)
三個	sānge	three (things)
四個	sz̀ge	four (things)

* 二 èr is the pure number, 兩 lyǎng is used for counting.

Pure Numbers:

今年是一九七三年.　　Jīnnyán shŕ yī-jyǒu-chī-sān nyán.
This year is 1973.

Number-Measure:

你有四個. 我有三個.　　 Nǐ yǒu sžge, wǒ yǒu sānge.
You have four, I have three.

The question-word jĭ 幾 meaning <u>how many</u>? is considered a number. It is used for quantities up to ten and can also be used with a measure.

幾個高. 幾個不高?　　Jĭge gāu, jĭge bù-gāu?

How many are tall, how many are not tall?

As for numbers higher than ten, counting **in Chinese** is like using an abacus. You say three-tens-one for thirty-one, seven-hundreds-five-tens-five for seven hundred fifty-five, and eight-thousands-seven-hundreds-four-tens-nine for eight thousand seven hundred forty-nine. One difference: the Chinese have a denomination ten-thousand which we do not. It is 萬 wàn. In Chinese, 77,000 is seven ten-thousands, seven thousands. The pattern is as follows, blanks left for the numbers one to nine:

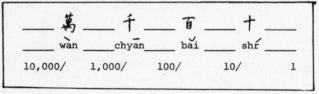

The two main patterns for numbers are: <u>Nu-M</u> for counting things, as in the examples above. And <u>Nu-M-N</u>, using single or several digit numbers to indicate the quantity of the noun.

我們有四個孩子.

Women you sɜge háidz.
We have four children.

<u>TIME-WORDS</u>: Indicators of time. Includes days of the week, months of the year, seasons. They can be either nouns or moveable adverbs. As nouns, they can be subjects or objects. As moveable adverbs, they may stand <u>before</u> or <u>after</u> the subject.

他昨天来.

Tā dzwótyān lái.
He came yesterday.

明年是一九七四年.

Míngnyán shr yī-jyǒu-chī-sɜ nyán.
Next year will be 1974.

<u>PLACE-WORDS</u>: The names of places. Can be names of cities and countries. Can be the subject or object of a sentence (acting as a noun) or the object of a co-verb (Chinese preposi- sitions). The three main co-verbs used with place-words are: 從 tsúng, <u>from</u>; 到 dàu, <u>to</u>; and 在 dzài, <u>in</u> or <u>at</u>. (See section on co-verbs.)

The specifiers jèi, <u>this</u>, nèi, <u>that</u>, and něi, <u>which</u>? become place-words by the addition of the particle 兒 er.

這兒	jèr	here (this place)
那兒	nèr	there (that place)
哪兒	nǎr	where? (which place?)

Some nouns (the names of places where people reside or carry on activity) are made into place-words by the addition of localizers, another phenomenon of Chinese grammar. Localizers locate objects or places in space. For example, the word _in_, when it follows a Chinese noun, makes it into a place-word. Thus it can follow the co-verbs named above, for they can take only a place-word, not just a simple noun.

家	jyā (N)	house
在家裡	dzài jyāli (PW)	in the house
學校	sywésyàu (N)	school
在學校裡	dzài sywésyàuli (PW)	in school

Add a localizer to a noun which is the name of a building or a place and you make it a place-word. Once a place-word, it can be the object of a co-verb, used as any other place-word.

LOCALIZERS conceptually indicate the space referred to, they indicate space very precisely. They follow nouns in the pattern: <u>N Loc</u>. Thus nouns can be converted to place-words when place-words are required in a pattern. Some localizers:

裡	-lǐ	in
外	-wài	outside
上	-shàng	above
下	-syà	below
左	-dzwǒ	left
右	-yòu	right
東	-dūng	east
南	-nán	south

| 西 | -syī | west |
| 北 | -beǐ | north |

門外	ménwài	outside the door
桌子上	jwōdzshàng	on the table
中國東部	Jūnggwōdūng	east of China

QUESTION-WORDS: These form a separate grammatical category in Chinese. The Chinese do not re-arrange a sentence to make a question as we do. They simply insert a question-word where they want the information supplied, leaving everything else the same. Thus, who? and what? function as nouns, what? can also be an adjective, how? and why? function as fixed adverbs, and where? will be the object of a co-verb. All convert a statement into a question.

誰	shéi	who?
誰說話？	shéi shwōhwà?	Who speaks?
我說話．	Wǒ shwōhwà.	I am speaking.

For further information, see Pattern Section.

All the preceding parts-of-speech are words used with nouns. All the following are words used with verbs.

ADVERBS modify verbs or other adverbs, as in English. There are two types in Chinese: Fixed and Moveable. Fixed adverbs (Adv) must precede the verb or another adverb.

MODYIFYING A STATIVE VERB:

這女孩子很好看．

Nyǔháidz hén hǎukàn.
The little girl is very pretty.

MODIFYING ANOTHER ADVERB:

這些男孩子都很高.

Nánháidz dōu hěn gāu.
The boys are all very tall.

The moveable adverb may precede the subject, as well as stand before the verb (abbreviated MA). All time-words are moveable adverbs.

上禮拜我看他.

Shànglìbài wǒ kàn tā.
I saw him last week.

CO-VERBS: These function like English prepositions. Most can be followed by a noun.

跟	gēn	with (a person)
用	yung	with(using an object for something)
給	gěi	to or for a person

A few must be followed by a place-word:

在	dzài	in, at
到	dàu	to (a place)
從	tsúng	from

Co-verbs precede the verb. If the sentence has a negative, it precedes the co-verb. If the sentence has an auxiliary verb, it precedes the co-verb. The pattern is:

N CV - N V

他跟他去.	Tā gēn tā chyù.	She left with him.
他對我說話.	Tā dwèi wǒ shwō-hwà.	He speaks to me.

POST-VERBS are "prepositions" which can follow certain
verbs, and which link the action of the verb to the object.
The two main post-verbs have already been introduced as co-verbs.
This is simply another function they have. They are: 在 dzài,
at or in; and 到 dàu, to (a place or time). These two post-
verbs can only be followed by place-words and time-words.

女孩子去到學校.   Nyǔháidz chyù dàu sywésyàu.
The little girl is going to school.

坐在這兒.   Dzwò dzài jèr.
Sit here.

PARTICLES are not full words. They are grammatical indi-
cators. They have no thought-content of their own and cannot
stand alone. They cannot be translated independently of the
word to which they are attached. The word 的 de, which
follows adjectives and clauses modifying nouns, is a particle.
Le 了 , which indicates the past tense, and yau 要 , which
indicates the future are also particles. Ma 嗎 , which is
a question-mark appearing at the end of a sentence, is a
particle.

This is a brief description of the principle parts-of-
speech in Chinese. What remains is to use these in sentences,
and to do that, patterns must be understood.

<u>PATTERNS</u>

Patterns are examples of the way Chinese sentences are constructed. Since word order is paramount and unvarying in Chinese, one simply has to learn the patterns, then substitute other words. Repetition is one of the great aids to committing these to memory, and the practice gained by substitution of other words from the Chinese section.

There are three basic things one should know to get on in a language: statements, questions and answers. The rest is refinements, trappings and other useful verbal paraphernalia. This is an attempt to provide the basics, a beginning.

<u>THE MOST SIMPLE SENTENCE</u>

This sentence pattern is notable for its appearance on grade-school blackboards. It is the same in Chinese as it is in English. Any noun, any verb.

<u>NOUN   VERB</u>

<u>SIMPLE DESCRIPTIVE SENTENCE</u>

More specifically, a sentence which describes something consists of a noun and a stative verb.

<u>N   SV</u>

| 山 高. | Shān gāu. | The mountain is tall. |
| 魚 小. | Yú syǎu. | The fish is small. |

First Variation: Negating the Basic Pattern

N   NEG   SV

山 不 高　　Shān bùgāu.　　The moutain is not tall.

魚 不 小　　yú búsyǎu.　　The fish is not small.

飯 不 好　　Fàn búhǎu.　　The food is not good.

Bu 不 is the Chinese negative meaning <u>not</u>. It can
precede any verb or an adverb. It pronounces in the 4th tone
unless the word following is also in the 4th tone. In this
case it pronounces in the 2nd tone. Reason: two successive
4th tones are hard to say, and not very pleasing to the Chinese
ear.

Second Variation: Adverb Added to the Basic Pattern

N   ADV   SV

你 很 好.　　Nǐ hén hǎu.　　You are very good.

你 不 很 好.　　Nǐ bùhén hǎu.　　You are not very good.

你 太 好.　　Nǐ tài hǎu.　　You are too good.

你 不 太 好.　　Nǐ bútài hǎu.　　You are not too good.

你 也 好.　　Nǐ yé hǎu.　　You too are good.

Third Variation: Combining the Positive and Negative

N   SV,   N   NEG   SV

我 好. 你 不 好.　　Wó hǎu, nǐ búhǎu.　　I'm good, but you aren't.

Either clause can come first. Conjunctions are rarely
used in Chinese, but they should be supplied to make smooth
English if necessary.

THE ACTION SENTENCE

This kind of sentence expresses action or occurrence, in contrast to the sentence which simply describes. The word order is exactly the same as English word order. The object is optional.

N V O

我們愛中國飯.
Wǒmen ài junggwó fàn.
We love Chinese food.

這個女孩子念書.
Jèige nyǔháidz nyanshū.
The little girl is studying.

THE SIMPLE QUESTION

The easiest way to form a question in Chinese: Take any statement with the basic pattern N V and add the interrogative particle ma 嗎 .

N V 嗎 ?

山高嗎?
Shān gāu ma?
Is the mountain tall?

孩子吃飯嗎?
Háidzmen chrfàn ma?
Are the children eating?

To answer positively, repeat the verb. Sometimes the adverb hen 很 , very is used. The answer translates, Yes.

山高嗎?　Shān gāu ma?　Is the mountain tall?
很高.　Hěn gāu.　Yes.

The negative answer is made by negating the verb, and translates, No.

這個馬大嗎?　Nèige mǎ dà ma?　Is that horse big?
不大.　Búdà.　No.

THE CHOICE QUESTION

The elegant choice question is one of the most beautiful formulations in all Chinese sentence-dom. The speaker gives a choice by using both the positive and negative form of the verb. The person addressed chooses an answer by using either the positive or negative form of the verb.

N V NEG V?

你要不要？
Ni yau buyau?
Do you want (it) or not?

我要．
Wo yau.
Yes, I want it.

不要．
Buyau.
No.

我們去不去
Women chyu buchyu?
Are we going or not?

去．
Chyu.
Yes.

不去．
Buchyu.
No.

Variation One: When the Verb has an Object

The object goes with the first verb, then the negative form of the verb follows.

N V O NEG V

你作飯不作？
Ni dzwofan budzwo?
Do you cook (or not)?

孩子愛書不愛？
Haidz ai shu buai?
Does the child like books or not?

Variation Two: Choice of Objects

When there is a choice between two objects, the verb
appears in the positive form with each of the objects. The
answer is the verb with the appropriate object.

N V O , V O ?

我們吃中國飯, ' Wǒmen chr jūnggwó fàn, chr
吃美國飯？ měigwo fàn?
Shall we eat Chinese or American
food?

我買書, 買報？ Wǒ mài shū, mài bàu?
Shall I buy a book or a newspaper?

買報. Mài bàu.
Buy a newspaper.

Variation Three: Choice of Subjects

Repeat the verb with each different subject.

N V , N₂ V?

你買, 我買？ Ni mǎi, wǒ mǎi?
Shall I buy it, or will you?

她來, 我來. Tā lái, wǒ lái?
Is she coming or am I?

QUESTION-WORD QUESTION

To form a question in English, one changes the word order
of the statement. The question word is brought to the beginning
of the sentence:

STATEMENT: He wants a book.

QUESTION: WHAT does he want?

The Chinese do not change the word order of the statement
at all, they simply put a question word where they want information.

STATEMENT: He wants a book.   Tā yàu <u>shū</u>.

QUESTION: WHAT does he want?   Tā yàu <u>shémma</u>?

The Question-Word as Subject:

QW (NEG) V (O)?

誰高？	Shéi gāu?	Who is tall?
誰不好？	Shéi bùhǎu?	Who is not good?
誰看書？	Shéi kànshū?	Who reads?
誰愛花？	Shéi aì hwà?	Who loves flowers?

Question-Word as Subject: Shemma? What?

甚麼對？	Shémma dwèi?	What is right?
甚麼字對？	Shémma dz dwèi?	Which character is right?
甚麼書好？	Shémma shū hǎu?	Which book is good?

Question-Word as Object: Shemma? What?

N V QW (N)?

你要甚麼？	Nǐ yàu shémma?	What do you want?
你要什麼書？	Nǐ yàu shémma shū?	Which book do you want?

Question-Word as Object: Dwoshau? How Much?

你有多少錢？	Nǐ yǒu dwoshǎu chyán?	
	How much money do you have?	

STATEMENTS, QUESTIONS AND ANSWERS:

	Pattern	Romanization
SIMPLE QUESTION		
Statement	N V	Tā hǎu.
Question	N V ?	Tā hǎu ma?
Answer	Adv. V	Hén hǎu.
		Bú hǎu.
CHOICE QUESTION		
Question	N V neg V?	Nǐ yàu bú yàu?
Question (with Object)	N V O neg V?	Nǐ kànshū búkàn?
Question	N V O_1 V O_2 ?	Nǐ kànshū, kànbàu?
Answer	V O_1 or V O_2	Kànshū/kànbàu.
QUESTION-WORD QUESTION		
Question	QW V?	Shéi shwōhwà?
Answer	N V	Wǒ shwōhwà.
Question	N V QW?	Tā jyàu shéi?
Answer	N V O	Tā jyàu tāde háidz.
Question	N V QW	Nǐ yàu shémma?
Answer	N V O	Wǒ yàu shū.

Chinese	English
他好.	He is good.
他好嗎?	Is he good?
很好	Yes.
不好	No.
你要不要?	Do you want (it)?
你看書不看?	Do you read books?
你看書,看報?	Do you read books or newspapers?
看書／看報	I read books./ I read newspapers.
誰說話?	Who is speaking?
我說話.	I am speaking.
他叫誰?	Whom is he calling?
他叫他的孩子	He calls his child.
你要什麼?	What do you want?
我要書.	I want a book.

THE PATTERNS IN BRIEF

SIMPLE SENTENCE	N V.
Negated	N 不 V.
Modified by Adverb	N Adv V.
Modified by Auxiliary Verb	N AV V.
SIMPLE SENTENCE WITH OBJECT	N V O.
Negated	N 不 V O.
Modified by Auxiliary Verb	N AV V O.
SIMPLE QUESTION	N V 嗎?
Negated	N 不 V 嗎?
Modified by Adverb	N Adv V 嗎?
Modified by Auxiliary Verb	N AV V 嗎?
With Object	N V O 嗎?
CHOICE QUESTION	N V 不 V?
With Object	N V O 不 V?
COMPOUND SENTENCE	N_1 V , N_2 V .
Negated	N_1 V , N_2 不 V
SIMPLE SENTENCE--PAST TENSE	N V 了.
With Object	N V O 了.
Negative Past Tense	N 沒 V.
Simple Past Tense Question	N V 了 嗎?
Negated	N 沒 V 嗎?
Choice Question--Past Tense	N V 了 沒 V?
SIMPLE SENTENCE WITH CO-VERB	N CV O V.
With Auxiliary Verb and Co-verb	N AV CV O V.
With Post-Verb	N V PV PW/TW.

NOUNS

A noun is usually modified by an adjective to gain variety
and depth of meaning. These are the ways to modify a noun.
Substitute any of these expressions in a pattern which calls
for a noun.

TO MODIFY A NOUN

When you wish to give to give a noun special characteris-
tics by modifying it with an adjective, use this pattern:

A 的 N

黑的馬	Hēide mǎ.	The black horse.
小的花	Syǎude hwā.	The small flower.

The particle de 的 , discussed above in parts-of-speech,
does not translate in English, but simply marks the modifier
in Chinese visually and aurally. A variety of this pattern is:

N V 的 N

我買的書.	Wǒ màide shū.	The book which I bought.
他寫的字.	Tā syěde dz.	The characters which she wrote.

This particle is also used to indicate the possessive:

N (or PN) 的 N

我的母親.	Wǒde mùchin.	My mother.
孩子的父親.	Háidzde fúchin.	The child's father.

AN EXCEPTION: Sometimes a noun can stand before another
noun and modify it without the particle de. This occurs frequently in the classical language, and in the colloquial language,
the most common examples are the name of a country preceding
another noun, and the names of close relatives.

美國書	Měigwó shū	An American book
中國人	Junggwó rén	A Chinese man
法國飯	Fàgwó fàn	French food
我(的)母親	Wǒ mǔchīn	My mother
他們(的)弟弟	Tāmen dìdì	Their little brother

WHEN TWO NOUNS ARE THE SUBJECT

This requires a special pattern in Chinese. Both nouns
are given followed by 都 dōu, all. Dou has a punctuating
effect indicating that what has gone before is the entire
subject. It only refers to what precedes it. The pattern is:

$$N_1 , N_2 \text{ 都 } V \text{ (O)}$$

山河都美麗.	Shān, hé dōu měilì. Both mountains and rivers are beautiful.
父母孩子都要吃飯.	Fùmǔ, háidz dōu yàu chrfàn. The parents and the child want to eat.

EMBELLISHING THE NOUN

A Chinese noun can be either singular or plural. The
character is the same, there is no special indication of number
as in English. But every noun is referred to by its own measure,
the name of a unit of the noun. One sheet of paper, one (sheet)
of painting. When there is no measure used in English, the

measure is simply not translated. With the measure, one uses
either a specifier (this refers to a specific noun) or a number
(this indicates an amount of the noun) or a specifier and a
number and a measure (this refers to a particular number of things).
To refer to a specific noun:

SP M N

這個人	Jèige rén	This man
那個人	Nèige rén	That man
哪個人?	Něige rén	Which man?
這本書	Jèibén shū	This book
那本書	Nèibén shū	That book
哪張畫兒?	Něijāng hwàr	Which painting?

To indicate a definite number of things, the Chinese use a
Number, a Measure and a Noun.

Nu M N

三個人	Sānge nyǔrén	Three women
五張桌子	Wǔjāng jwōdz	Five tables
七位先生	Chīwèi syānshēng	Seven gentlemen

To indicate a specific definite number of things, the
two patterns are combined. The words then appear in this order:

SP Nu M N

这三本书   Jèi sānběn shū
These three books

那五個孩子   Nèi wǔge háidz
Those five children

哪七位先生?   Něi chiwèi syānshēng
Which seven gentlemen?

If one wishes to indicate possession in the above pattern, the possessive comes first:

我这三本书   Wǒ jèi sānběn shū
These three books of mine

他那五個孩子   Tā nèi wǔge háidz
Those five children of hers

NOTE: There is no definite article in Chinese comparable to the English the. Jeige is used so frequently in colloquial speech that often it serves as a definite article and translates so.

VERBS

Some elaborations on the basic verb.

AUXILIARY VERBS

Certain Chinese verbs are called auxiliary verbs simply because they precede other verbs. They are just like English auxiliary verbs.

愛	ài	to like, love
可以	kéyi	may, can
能	néng	be able to
得	děi	must
要	yàu	want

Use them according to this pattern. If the negative is
needed, it precedes the auxiliary verb.

N (NEG) AV V

你可以走.
Nǐ kéyǐ dzǒu.
You may leave.

他不要吃飯.
Tā búyàu chrfàn.
He doesn't want to eat.

EXPRESSING THE PAST

To express the past, use the particle le 了 . When le
follows a verb, it indicates the past tense. The pattern is:

N V 了 (O)

我說了.
Wǒ shwōle.
I said it.

他吃了很多.
Tā chrle hěn dwō.
She ate a lot of food.

你吃了嗎?
Nǐ chrle ma?
Have you eaten?

To express the negative in the past, use méi 沒 , instead
of bù 不 .

N 沒 V (O)

昨天我父親沒
Dzwótyan wǒ fùchīn meilai.
My father didn't come yesterday.

他去年沒念書.
Tā chyùnyán méinyánshū.
He didn't study last year.

For the simple question, the particle ma is simply added to
the statement which is in the past tense. Then the question is

also in the past tense:

你念了這本書嗎?　　　Nǐ nyánle jèibén shū ma?
　　　　　　　　　　　Did you read this book?

The choice question is formed in the same way, but both the positive and negative forms of the verb must be in the past tense. The pattern is:

N　V　LE , MÉIYOU?

你吃了飯沒有?　　　Nǐ chrle fàn méiyǒu?
　　　　　　　　　Have you eaten?

吃了.　　　　　　Chrle.
　　　　　　　　Yes.

沒吃飯.　　　　　Méichrfàn.
　　　　　　　　No.

他走了沒有?　　　Tā dzǒule méiyǒu?
　　　　　　　　Did he leave?

走了.　　　　　　Dzǒule.
　　　　　　　　Yes.

沒走.　　　　　　Méidzǒu.
　　　　　　　　No.

EXPRESSING THE FUTURE

The English future tense WILL + VERB (as in will go) has an exact equivalent in Chinese. The pattern is:

N　(NEG)　YAU　V　(O)

我要來.　　　　　　Wǒ yàu lái.
　　　　　　　　　I will come.

明天我們要去.　　　Míngtyān wǒmen yàu chyù.
　　　　　　　　　Tomorrow we will go.

孩子明年不要上學.　Háidz míngnyán búyàu shàngsywé.
　　　　　　　　　The child will not go to school
　　　　　　　　　next year.

CO-VERBS

Co-verbs are the equivalent of English prepositions. The pattern for all co-verbs is:

N CV O V

Each Chinese co-verb has a special use. Gěi 給 is used for indirect objects and translates to. Dwèi 對 is used with verbs meaning to speak, and also translates to. It literally means to face, and a sentence such as Wǒ dwèi nǐ shwōhwà would literally translate "I face you and speak" while the common translation is "I am speaking to you." The co-verb gēn 跟 is the same as the English with when it means "accompanied by."

他母親給他作飯.
Tā muchin gěi tā dzwòfàn.
His mother cooks for him.

那個中國人給我一本書.
Nèige jūnggwò rén gěi wǒ yìběn shū.
That Chinese man gave me a book.

你對他們說中國話,
　對我們說英文.
Nǐ dwèi tāmen shwō jūnggwò hwà, dwèi wǒmen shwō yingwén.
You speak Chinese to them, but speak English to us.

他跟我念書.
Tā gēn wǒ nyánshū.
He studies with me.

你跟誰住?
Nǐ gēn shéi jù?
With whom are you living?

VERBS OF MOTION AND THEIR CO-VERBS

The verbs of motion, lái 來 to come, and chyù 去 to go, take special co-verbs. There are three:

坐	dzwó	by (means of)
從	tsúng	from
到	dàu	to

Dzwó is used to indicate the means of transportation, tsúng indicates the place _from_ which the traveller departs, and dàu indicates the place _to_ which he is going. The word order is a great example of Chinese logic: first you "sit" in a means of conveyance (the literal meaning of dzwó is _sit_) then you begin _from_ one place and end at the destination (the literal meaning of dàu is _arrive_). These co-verbs may be used separately or in combination, but if more than one is used, this order must be strictly observed.

N CV N lái

他坐汽車來.
Tā dzwó chìchē lái.
He is coming by car.

他從他的家裡來.
Tā tsúng tāde jyālǐ lái.
He is coming from his house.

他到這兒來.
Tā dàu jèr lái.
He is coming here.

N CV N chyù

他坐船去.
Tā dzwó chwán chyù.
She is going by boat.

他從美國去.
Tā tsúng Měigwó chyù.
She is going from America.

她到中國去.　　　　Tā dàu jūnggwó chyù.
　　　　　　　　　　She is going to China.

SUMMARY OF PATTERNS:

                          lái
              N CV N chyù

N	dzwó	N	V		Subject coming/going by (conveyance)
N	tsúng	PW	V		Subject coming/going from (place)
N	dàu	PW	V		Subject coming/going to (place)

When these co-verbs are used in combination, the order
must be observed because it is strictly in keeping with Chinese
logic, which is the mainstay of Chinese grammar. When all
three co-verbs are used, the pattern looks like this:

                                          lái
         N dzwó O tsúng PW dàu PW chyù

他坐汽車從他的家裡
到這兒來.

Tā dzwó chīchē tsúng tāde jyālǐ
dàu jèr lái.
He is coming here from his house
by car.

他坐船從美國到中國去.

Tā dzwó chwán tsúng Měigwó dàu
jūnggwó chyù.
She is going by boat from America
to China.

我的朋友坐火車從舊金山
到我家裡來了.

Wǒde péngyou dzwó hwǒchē tsúng
Jyóujīnshān dàu wǒ jyālǐ láile.
My friend came to my house
from San Francisco by train.

POST-VERBS

These are prepositions which follow the verb. There are
two: dzài 在 , and dàu 到 . Dzài means to be in, on, or at.
It can also stand as a full verb. It is always followed by a
place-word. As a full verb, it is used in this pattern:

N dzài PW

王太太在家裡.　Wàng tàitai dzài jyālǐ.
　　　　　　　Mrs. Wang is in the house.

我家城外頭.　Wǒde sywésyàu dzài chéngwài.
　　　　　　　My school is outside the city.

... 在城裡.　. . . dzài chénglǐ
　　　　　　　My school is north of the city.

... 在城北.　. . . dzài chéngběi.
　　　　　　　My school is south of the city.

... 在城中.　. . . dzài chéngjūng.
　　　　　　　My school is in the center of
　　　　　　　the city.

Another pattern for expressing location:

PW yǒu N

桌子上有書.　Jwōdzshàng yǒu shū.
　　　　　　　There are books on the table.

這兒有山.　Jèr yǒu shān.
　　　　　　　There are mountains here.

那兒有河.　Nèr yǒu jāng.
　　　　　　　There are rivers there.

A post-verb is a verbal element added to some, not all,
action verbs, which links the action of the main verb to the
object which follows it. Both dzài and dàu can be post-verbs.
Sometimes going from Chinese to English, they are not translated
because to do so would be redundant. But they make perfect
sense to the eye, and to the Chinese penchant for verbal logic.

N V dzài PW

他住在我家裡.　Tā jùdzài wǒ jyālǐ.
　　　　　　　He lives in my house.

他們坐在那兒，
我坐在哪兒？

Tāmen dzwódzài ner. Wǒ dzwódzài nǎr?
They are sitting there. Where shall I sit?

Dàu may take a time-word or a place-word as its object.

			PW/
N	V	dàu	TW

他到北京去.

Tā chyùdàu Beijīng.
She is going to Peking.

她走到學校.

Tā dzǒudàu sywésyàu.
She walks to school.

她念到夜裡.

Tā nyándàu yelǐ.
She studies until evening.

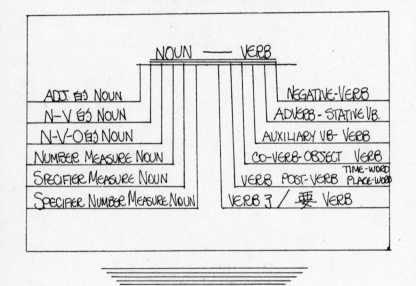

BASIC SENTENCE PATTERN
WITH VARIATIONS

NOUN — VERB

ADJ. 的 NOUN	NEGATIVE-VERB
N-V 的 NOUN	ADVERB - STATIVE VB.
N-V-O 的 NOUN	AUXILIARY VB- VERB
NUMBER MEASURE NOUN	CO-VERB-OBJECT VERB
SPECIFIER MEASURE NOUN	VERB POST-VERB TIME-WORD PLACE-WORD
SPECIFIER NUMBER MEASURE NOUN	VERB 了 / 要 VERB

Brushes for Painting
and Calligraphy (Laura DeCoppet)

The Four Treasures of the Scholar's Table (Laura DeCoppet)

CHINESE

" . . . language, like the ancient Chinese script, should be able to express the most complex matters graphically, without excluding individual imagination and inventiveness."

Hermann Hesse, The Glass Bead Game, 27.

"The sum of human wisdom is not contained in any one language, and no single language is capable of expressing all forms and degrees of human comprehension."

Ezra Pound, ABC of Reading, 34.

THE
CHINESE
VIEW
OF
THINGS

<u>THE BEGINNING</u>

From the One, the Great Ultimate, the Formless, the Unbounded, the Mother of all things . . . came the Two.

THE GREAT ULTIMATE   TAI JI

THE TWO   YIN AND YANG

Yin, the Female, the Receptive, Earth, Darkness, and Yang,
the Male, the Active, Heaven, Light. Their symbol is 🌓 .
From the intercourse of these Two came . . .

THE 10,000 THINGS   WAN WU

All forms of life, the phenomena of nature.

THE WAY OF NATURE

For the ancient Chinese, the elements were five forces in
an eternal cycle of creation and destruction. Wood creates
fire, fire produces earth, earth produces metal, or, in reverse,
water extinguishes fire, fire melts metal, metal cuts wood.
The directions, the seasons, the colors, the activities of life,
the parts of the body, all corresponded to these five elements.
These correspondences were the expression of universal harmony.
The sage, the king, the physician, the farmer, all order their
activities according to this cycle, thus achieving oneness with
the harmony of nature. (<u>Chinese</u> <u>Folk</u> <u>Medicine</u>, 3.)

THE FIVE ELEMENTS

WOOD   MÙ   NOUN

This is a drawing of a tree. The vertical stroke is the
trunk. The horizontal stroke is the branches. The sweeping
strokes are the roots. 林 , two trees, means <u>forest</u>. Three
trees, 森 , means <u>thicket</u>.

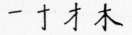

FIRE   HWǑ   NOUN

This drawing has the jumping dancing quality of fire. The
ancient drawing was 山 . Two fires, 炎 , means <u>brilliant</u>.

、 丿 火 火

METAL   JĪN   NOUN

The old drawing 金 , shows layers of metal concealed under
the earth.

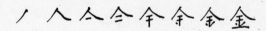

WATER   SHWĔI   NOUN

The ancient word is  , a drawing of a stream.

丿 亅 オ 扌 水

EARTH   TŬ   NOUN

The ancient character is Ω , a drawing of the phallic-
shaped altar of the soil.

一 十 土

THE FIVE DIRECTIONS

EAST	DŪNG	LOCALIZER

This character is a picture of sunrise. The sun is seen at the horizon between the branches and roots of a tree, 東. By extension it came to mean East, since that is where the sun rises.

SOUTH	NÁN	LOCALIZER

西

WEST	HSĪ	LOCALIZER

一 丆 冂 両 西 西

北

NORTH	BĚI	LOCALIZER

一 十 北 北 北

CENTER   JŪNG   LOCALIZER

This is a drawing of a target pierced in its center by
an arrow.

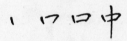

GREEN   CHĪNG   STATIVE VERB, ADJECTIVE

The old drawing was 靑. The bottom shows a square container, a dot indicating its colored contents. Above, 主 serves as the phonetic.

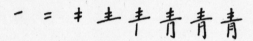

RED   CHÌR   STATIVE VERB, ADJECTIVE

This has an exciting old drawing: 炎 , a picture of a man above a fire 火.

一 十 土 十 赤 赤 赤

WHITE BÁI STATIVE VERB, ADJECTIVE

The drawing was a <u>loan</u> from an identical <u>sounding</u> word.
It has nothing to do with the meaning, <u>white</u>. This is Radical
106, and appears as a sense-element in many words.

BLACK HĒI STATIVE VERB, ADJECTIVE

Originally 炎 , a drawing of a human face and body covered
with spots, possibly warpaint. This character is Radical 203.

丨 冂 冂 冂 四 四 甲 里 里 黑 黑 黑

YELLOW   HWÁNG   STATIVE VERB/ADJECTIVE

Yellow was the imperial color of China for thousands of years. This character is Radical 201 and appears in other words as a sense-indicator.

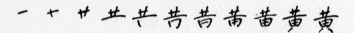

THE FIVE SEASONS

| SPRING | CHWŪN TYĀN | NOUN/TIME-WORD |

The Spring and Autumn Annals tells how the emperor conforms
to the way of nature: "During the three spring months, the
emperor remains in the eastern wing of the Hall of Light. He
rides in a carriage drawn by green-shimmering dragon horses.
All the banners are green. His officials and entourage are
dressed in green gowns and wear green jade jewelry. The emperor
conducts the sacrificial rites on the palace's east lawn. He
orders his ministers to be magnanimous and to exercise gentleness,
and to prevent the felling of trees and the taking up of arms."
(quoted in Chinese Folk Medicine, 5.)

Tyān appears in all the names of the seasons. Usually it
means day, but here it means time.

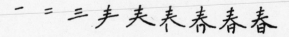

SUMMER   SYÀ TYĀN   NOUN/TIME-WORD

"During the three summer months, the emperor confines himself
to the southern wing of the Hall of Light. His carriage is
drawn by fox-red horses. The banners are red. The emperor's
staff are clad in red robes and wear red jade. Sacrificial
rites are conducted on the south lawn. The emperor orders his
ministers to nominate worthy persons for awards and medals and
to urge the populace to apply themselves to their tasks with
vigor." (Chinese Folk Medicine,5)

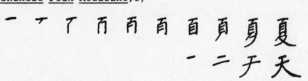

FALL   CHYŌU TYĀN   NOUN/TIME-WORD

"During the three autumn months, the emperor stays in the
western wing of the Hall of Light. His war-carriage is drawn
by white horses. The banners are white. His officials wear
white gowns and white jade jewels. He conducts sacrificial
rites on the palace's west lawn. The emperor orders his ministers to revise the laws and to conduct the court trials.
Dressed in his war habit, the emperor personally takes part in
the hunting expeditions." (from the Spring and Autumn Annals
quoted in Chinese Folk Medicine, 6.)

The character for fall is made of 禾 corn and 火 fire.
Indian summer is considered a separate season, corresponding
to the fifth color, fifth element and fifth direction.

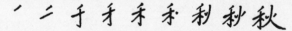

WINTER   DŪNG TYĀN   NOUN/TIME-WORD

"During the three winter months, the emperor confines himself
to the north wing of the Hall of Light. He rides a black carriage
drawn by black horses. The banners are black. His staff wears
black robes and black jade. Sacrificial rites are observed on
the north lawn. The emperor orders his ministers to replenish
the storage vaults and to have all necessary repairs done on
doors and locks. On the eve of the New Year, the exorcisers
are called for to expel the spirits of pestilence." (<u>Chinese</u>
<u>Folk</u> <u>Medicine</u>, 6.)

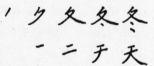

THE CHINESE PHILOSOPHERS

LAU TZU   LǍU TZU

The Old Master. Acknowledged as the
founder of Taoism, the philosophy of
the Way.

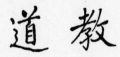

THE WAY   DÀU

Written of in the <u>Dau De Ching</u>, the
book attributed to Lau Tzu.

TAOISM   DÀUJYÀU

The teaching of the Way.

孔
夫
子

CONFUCIUS KǓNG FŪ TZǓ

The founder of the ethical and moral philosophy named Confucianism, after him, for centuries the philosophical backbone of the Chinese empire. The name Confucius is a Jesuit Latinization of the Chinese name.

孔 教

CONFUCIANISM KUNG JYÀU

The teaching of Confucius: filial piety, reciprocity, behavior according to rites.

THE SUPERIOR MAN   JYŪN DǮ

The Princely Man, the Sage, who is the model of behavior in the Confucian Classics.

THE INFERIOR MAN   SYĂU RÉN

The Small or Ignoble Man, the negative example in the Confucian Classics.

BUDDHA   FWO   NOUN

   Buddha was a perfectly realized Indian teacher, not a
Chinese properly speaking. Still, his teaching took hold in
China and had profound influence in arts, letters and even
politics. The teaching was refined by the Chinese mind, so
that in China, Buddhism is unmistakably Chinese.

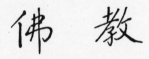

BUDDHISM   FWÓ-JYÀU   NOUN

"The teachings of Buddha."

NOUNS:
HEAVEN
EARTH
MAN

HEAVEN

THE SUN   R̀   NOUN

This character comes from an ancient drawing of the sun which looked like this ⊙ . It also means <u>day</u>. These two characters are beautiful examples of how Chinese characters, as they were handed down through the centuries changed from round primitive designs to stylized square designs, yet still retaining the same basic idea.

丿 冂 月 日

THE MOON   YWÈ   NOUN

This drawing was originally a crescent moon 𝌽 . China traditionally used the lunar calendar and counted months by moon cycles. So 月 also means month.

丿 刀 月 月

THE CHINESE ZODIAC

All names of animals, unlike our zodiac, and all beautiful characters.

THE RAT   SHǓ   NOUN

ARIES. This character, Radical 208, shows the rat's head 臼 , his legs 比 , and his tail ⟍ .

THE OX   NYǓ   NOUN

TAURUS. The ancient drawing was an ox's face and horns ψ .

虎

THE TIGER   HŬ   NOUN

GEMINI. The old drawing was a picture of a tiger on its hind legs with its claws out .

丿 ⺊ ⺊ 广 卢 虍 虎 虎

兔

THE HARE   TÙ   NOUN

CANCER.

丿 ⺅ 匀 白 夕 兔 兔

THE DRAGON   LÚNG   NOUN

LEO. The dragon was the imperial emblem,
just as the lion is the regal emblem in
our zodiac.

龍

THE SNAKE   SHÉ   NOUN

VIRGO. The radical 虫 was originally
 , a picture of a cobra with its
hood spread.

蛇

馬

THE HORSE MǍ NOUN

LIBRA. A very good drawing of a horse.
F is the neck with mane flying, ⊐
is the back and tail, ⼋⼁ are the four
legs.

丨 厂 厂 厈 厈 馬 馬
馬 馬 馬

羊

THE SHEEP YÁNG NOUN

SCORPIO. The old drawing was a
picture of the sheep's face and his
big horns: 苂 . This is Radical 123.

丶 ⼧ ⼳ ⼳ 兰 羊

THE MONKEY   HÓU   NOUN

SAGITARRIUS.

猴

THE COCK   JĪ   NOUN

CAPRICORN. The right part 隹 , is a
drawing of a <u>short-tailed bird</u>. The
ancient drawing was 瞿 . 爪 is a
picture of a bird-claw.

雞

狗

THE DOG   GŎU   NOUN

AQUARIUS. The left part is a drawing
of a dog 犭, in its abbreviated
form 犭. 句 is a phonetic.

ノ 犭 犭 犭 犳 狗 狗 狗
狗

豬

THE BOAR   JŪ   NOUN

PISCES. 豕 is a drawing of a pig
and 者 is a phonetic.

一 丆 丆 豸 豸 豕
豕 豕 豕 豕 豺 豺
豬 豬 豬

STARS AND PLANETS

STAR   SYĪNG   NOUN

This drawing is a sun 日 above the radical 生 which means <u>birth</u>. Thus, a star is a <u>sun-birth</u>. The ancient character is a drawing of a constellation ♉ .

丶　口　日　日　尸　昂　昂　星　星

MERCURY   SHWĔI-SYĪNG   NOUN

The Water-Star. The first five planets bear the names of the five elements.

VENUS   JĪN-SYĪNG   NOUN

The Gold-Star.

火星

MARS   HWŎ-SYĪNG   NOUN

The Fire Star.

木星

JUPITER   MŬ-SYĪNG   NOUN

The Wood Star.

土星

SATURN   TŬ-SYĪNG   NOUN

The Earth Star.

URANUS   TYĀN WÁNG SYĪNG   NOUN

The Sky-King Star.

天
王
星

NEPTUNE   HǍI WÁNG SYĪNG   NOUN

The Sea-King Star.

海
王
星

PLUTO   MÍNG WÁNG SYĪNG   NOUN

King of the Underworld Star.

冥
王
星

WATER

雨

RAIN   **YŴÉ**   **NOUN**

The oldest form of this word shows a cloud with drops of
water falling: .

一 丆 丆 币 雨 雨 雨 雨

海

SEA   **HǍI**   **NOUN**

The water radical at the left, the phonetic at the right.
Shānghǎi, 上海, "on the sea."

RIVER   HÉ   **NOUN**

A small river. The left part is the sense-indicator, <u>water</u>. The right part is the phonetic.

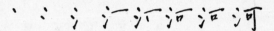

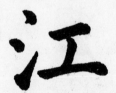

RIVER   JĀNG   **NOUN**

A big river. The Yangtze is Yang Jang, 長江. Again, the left is the water radical, the right is the phonetic.

150

OCEAN   YÁNG   NOUN

Again, 氵 , water, as the sense-indicator and 羊 yang
as the phonetic.

丶 丶 氵 氵 氵 氵 氵 洋 洋

大 西 洋

ATLANTIC OCEAN   DÀ SYĪ YÁNG

"The Great Western Ocean."

太 平 洋

PACIFIC OCEAN   TÀI PÍNG YÁNG

"The Very Peaceful Ocean."

LAKE   HŪ   NOUN

Water is the radical, abbreviated 氵 and 胡, <u>hu</u>, is
the phonetic.

丶 丶 氵 氵 汁 汁 沽 沽 泐 湖 湖 湖

湖 北

HUBEI   HÚBĚI   PLACE-WORD

The name of a province in China meaning <u>north</u> <u>of</u> <u>the</u> <u>lake</u>.

湖 南

HUNAN   HÚNÁN   PLACE-WORD

Another Chinese province. The name means <u>south</u> <u>of</u> <u>the</u> <u>lake</u>.

RICE   MĬ   NOUN

The ancient drawing was a picture of a rice paddy, ⊞ . This is the word for uncooked rice. The word for cooked rice is <u>fan</u>, 飯 .

`、　丶丷丷半米米`

BAMBOO   JŬ   NOUN

This character comes from an ancient drawing of bamboo which looked like this: 竹 . It shows the characteristic hanging leaves.

`ノ　ト　ケ　竹　竹　竹`

GRASS   **TSǍU**   **NOUN**

At the top of this character is the abbreviation of the
grass radical 艸, a drawing of plants. The bottom part
is the phonetic dzau.

丶 丷 艹 艹 艹 芐 芐 苩 苩 草 草

FLOWER   **HWĀ**   **NOUN**

The grass radical (#140) is at the top again, with the
phonetic hwa at the bottom.

丶 丷 艹 艹 艹 艻 花 花

EARTH   TŬ   NOUN

石

STONE   **SHŔ**   **NOUN**

This is a picture of a cliff and a falling rock   from
the ancient drawing  .

一 厂 プ 石 石

山

MOUNTAIN   **SHĀN**   **NOUN**

The ancient picture was a drawing of a mountain range,  .
The modern drawing is the same, reduced to an abstract representation.

丨 凵 山

MAN

人

MAN RÉN NOUN

This is a drawing of a man walking. It can mean human being. It is Radical 9, and when it appears at the left side of a word, it is written 亻.

丿 人

女

WOMAN NYǓ NOUN

From the ancient drawing . This is Radical 38.

く 夂 女

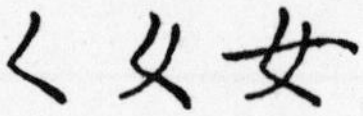

MALE, MAN NÁNRÉN NOUN

力 is strength, 田 is a field. Maleness
is strength in the fields. This is the
modern expression for man.

丨 冂 日 田 田 男 男

男人

FEMALE, WOMAN NYŬRÉN NOUN

It is almost as if the word 人 has no
gender, and the prefixes distinguish
between the different sexes of the species.
This is the modern expression for woman.

女人

BOY NÁNHÁIDZ NOUN

男孩子

GIRL NYŬHÁIDZ NOUN

女孩子

CHILD   **HÁIDZ**   **NOUN**

In the first and second characters, 子 is a drawing of a
baby. In ancient times, it was written 우 . In the first
character, 亥 is for sound only.

THE FAMILY

FATHER FÙCHĪN **NOUN**

The ancient drawing for <u>fu</u> is 予 , which shows a hand holding the ancestral tablet. The father's duty was to carry on the line of his ancestors. ╯ 八 少 父

丶 ㅗ ㅗ ㅗ 立 立 辛 辛

亲 亲 亲 新 親 親 親 親

母 親

MOTHER MŬCHĪN **NOUN**

The ancient word is exactly the same as that for <u>woman</u> but the breasts are marked by dots: 夷 . Thus, the idea of bearing and nurturing children is embodied in the concept.

The Chinese have names for every conceivable family relation, for different kinds and degrees of cousins, in-laws and elders. These are the names for children in the immediate family.

ELDER SISTER   JYÉJYĚ   NOUN

ㄑ ㄠ 女 女﹀ 奶 奶 姐 姐

YOUNGER SISTER   MÈIMÈI   NOUN

ㄑ ㄠ 女 女 女﹀ 女二 妹 妹 妹

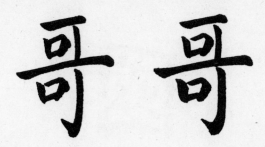

ELDER BROTHER　　　　　GĒGE　　　　　NOUN

一 丆 石 石 可 哥 哥 哥 哥 哥

弟 弟

YOUNGER BROTHER　　　　　DÌDÌ　　　　　NOUN

丶 丷 丷 弟 弟 弟 弟 弟

SOCIETY

COUNTRY/NATION   GWÓ   NOUN

This is <u>country</u> in the oldest sense of the word. It shows
the army, symbolized by the dagger axe 戈 , in command,
symbolized by a mouth 口 , of the borders, represented by
口 , an enclosure.

丨 冂 冂 冂 同 同 同 同 國 國 國 國

中 國   CHINA   JŪNGGWÓ   NOUN
         "The Middle Kingdom," an ancient name.

日 本   JAPAN   RBÈN   NOUN
         "The Land of the Rising Sun." The
         Japanese pronounce these characters Nippon.

AMERICA   MĔIGWÓ   NOUN

"The Beautiful Country." The Chinese way
of naming foreign countries is to match a
syllable of their own to the first syllable
of the Western name, and choose a favorable
character.

美國

ENGLAND   YĪNGGWÓ   NOUN

"The Brave Country." The Chinese syllable
<u>ying</u> is the closest to the <u>Eng</u> in England.

英國

FRANCE   FĂGWÓ   NOUN

"The Lawful Country."

法國

GERMANY   DÉGWÓ   NOUN

"The Virtuous Country," from the first
syllable of Deutschland.

德國

CITY   CHÉNG   NOUN

Earth, 土 , is the radical and <u>cheng</u> 成 the phonetic.

一 十 土 圹 圹 坊 城 城 城

北 京

PEKING   BĚIJĪNG   PLACE-WORD

"The Northern Capitol."

南 京

NANKING   NÁNJĪNG   PLACE-WORD

"The Southern Capitol."

丶 亠 六 古 古 宁 京 京

HOUSE JYA NOUN

A house is a pig 豕 under a roof 宀 . When the localizer
li 裡 follows any of these words, the noun becomes a place-word,
and so can follow a co-verb. In the house, dzài jyālǐ, 在家裡.

丶 丨 丷 宀 宀 宀 宍 家 家 家

SCHOOL SYWÉSYÀU NOUN

RESTAURANT   **FÀNGWǍR**   **NOUN**

我們去到飯館兒   Wǒmen chyù dàu fàngwǎrlǐ.

We're going to the restaurant.

CONVEYANCES

VEHICLE, CART   CHÉ   NOUN

This is a drawing of a cart seen from above: the vertical line is the axle, the top and bottom lines are the wheels, the square in the center is the body of the cart.

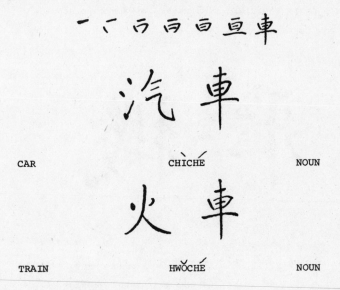

CAR   CHICHÉ   NOUN

TRAIN   HWŎCHÉ   NOUN

These names for means of transportation are used with the verbs of motion, _to come_ and _to go_, and the co-verb dzwó, "by means of." See Grammar Section.

BOAT   CHWĀN   NOUN

The left part is a picture of a boat turned on its side: 舟 . The right part is a picture of a marsh between mountains 㕣 , possibly the waterway the boat travels on.

PLANE   FĒIJĪ   NOUN

"A flying machine." The first word, _to fly_, is a picture of wings with feathers. The second word means _machine_.

THREE GENERAL NOUNS

東西

THING   DŪNGSYĪ   NOUN

     This is a compound made of opposites.
This kind of combination is quite
common in Chinese. Literally, this
word is <u>east and west</u>.

地方

PLACE   DÌFĀNG   NOUN

     This is a synonym compound, also
very common in Chinese. 土 means
earth, and has 土 the earth radical,
plus 也 for sound. 方 means place,
Radical 70.

時候

TIME   SHÍHÒU   NOUN

丨 丗 日 日 日一 日十 旪 旪 時 時

丿 亻 亻 仁 仴 仴 侯 侯 侯 候

NOW   SYÀNDZÀI   TIME-WORD/
                                                     MOVEABLE ADVERB

This word, as a moveable adverb, can come before or after

the subject.

DAY   TYĀN   NOUN

   This word also means <u>heaven</u>, the god of the ancient Chinese.
This is an anthropomorphic god, conceived as a big man, his
arms outstretched, his head touching heaven.

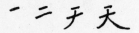

SOME EXPRESSIONS (All Moveable Adverbs):

今	天	JĪNTYĀN	TODAY
明	天	MÍNGTYĀN	TOMORROW
昨	天	DZWÓTYĀN	YESTERDAY
每	天	TYĀNTYĀN	EVERY DAY

NIGHT   YÈ   NOUN

This word was borrowed to write <u>night</u>, a "loan word."
It has nothing to do with the meaning.

丶　亠　广　疒　夜　夜　夜　夜

一　夜

THE WHOLE NIGHT   Ī YÈ   ADVERB

YEAR   NYÁN   NOUN

This word was originally drawn 夫 , a picture of a man carrying grain. It meant <u>harvest</u>. The year is marked from harvest to harvest in an agricultural society, so this word came to mean <u>year</u> by extension.

Years are written in single numbers. 1973 is 一九七三年. yī-jyòu-chī-sān nyán.

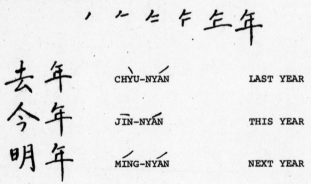

去年   CHYÙ-NYÁN   LAST YEAR

今年   JĪN-NYÁN   THIS YEAR

明年   MÍNG-NYÁN   NEXT YEAR

MONTH		YWÈ	NOUN

A drawing of the moon 𝄐 . China uses the lunar calendar. From any phase of the moon to the same phase is a <u>moon-th</u>.

<u>MONTHS</u> <u>OF</u> <u>THE</u> <u>YEAR</u>:

一	月	Yī-ywè	JANUARY
二	月	Èr-ywè	FEBRUARY
三	月	Sān-ywè	MARCH
四	月	Sz̀-ywè	APRIL
五	月	Wǔ-ywè	MAY
六	月	Lyòu-ywè	JUNE
七	月	Chī-ywè	JULY
八	月	Bā-ywè	AUGUST
九	月	Jyǒu-ywè	SEPTEMBER
十	月	Shŕ-ywè	OCTOBER
十一	月	Shŕ-yī-ywè	NOVEMBER
十二	月	Shŕ-èr-ywè	DECEMBER

DAY OF THE MONTH   HÀU   MEASURE

This word is comparable to the <u>-st</u> in <u>first</u> of the month,
or the <u>-th</u> in <u>fifteenth</u>. It is used to write dates:

一九七三年(year)   六月 (month)   一號 (day)

You can see the date in a Chinese painting to the left of the
poem or quotation, after the painter's seal, written vertically.

一 號   First (of the month)

二 號   Second

三 號   Third

WEEK   LǏ-BÀI   NOUN

The days of the week are made by combining the word
li-bai with the numbers one to six, and then the Chinese sun,
for Sunday.

禮拜一	Lǐ-bài-yī	MONDAY
禮拜二	Lǐ-bài-èr	TUESDAY
禮拜三	Lǐ-bài-sān	WEDNESDAY
禮拜四	Lǐ-bài-sz̀	THURSDAY
禮拜五	Lǐ-bài-wǔ	FRIDAY
禮拜六	Lǐ-bài-lyòu	SATURDAY
禮拜日	Lǐ-bài-r̀	SUNDAY

I, ME   WǑ   PERSONAL PRONOUN

This shows a hand 手 , anciently written 𐆥 , holding a
weapon. It is a symbol for <u>ego</u>.

ˊ 手 手 手 手 我 我 我

YOU   NǏ   PERSONAL PRONOUN

ˊ 亻 亻ˊ 亻ˊ 你 你 你

HE/SHE and HIM/HER   TĀ   PERSONAL PRONOUN

She is also written 她 (tā). The woman radical replaces
the man radical.

ˊ 亻 亻 他 他

The plural of all these pronouns is formed the same way, by adding the particle <u>men</u>, 們 , which has a neutral tone.

| WE, US | WŎMEN | PERSONAL PRONOUN |

| YOU | NĬMEN | PERSONAL PRONOUN |

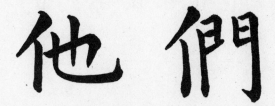

| THEY, THEM | TĀMEN | PERSONAL PRONOUN |

The plural for a group of women would be <u>tāmen</u>, 她們 .

ノ 亻 亻 亻 亻 伊 伊 伊 們

THE PARTICLE WHICH SIGNIFIES THAT A GROUP OF WORDS
MODIFIES A NOUN

DE   PARTICLE

This is used in the pattern ADJ 的 NOUN. See Grammar
Section for examples.

很大的書   Hěn dàde shū.   A very big book.

ㄟ ㄟ 白 白 白 的 的

NUMBERS

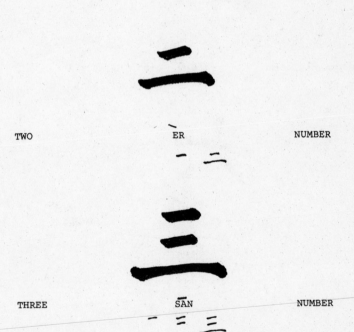

ONE   YĪ   NUMBER

The horizontal stroke should be bone-shaped, thicker at the ends, slender at the center.

TWO   ÈR   NUMBER

THREE   SĀN   NUMBER

四

| FOUR | SZ̀ | NUMBER |

五

| FIVE | WŬ | NUMBER |

六

| SIX | LYÒU | NUMBER |

七

SEVEN　　　　　CHĪ　　　　　NUMBER

一七

八

EIGHT　　　　　BĀ　　　　　NUMBER

八八

九

NINE　　　　　JYÒU　　　　　NUMBER

丿九

TEN	SHŔ	NUMBER

PURE NUMBERS

For years, telephone, pure counting, mathematics.

一	Yī	One
二	Èr	Two
三	Sān	Three
四	Sz̀	Four
五	Wǔ	Five
六	Lyòu	Six
七	Chī	Seven
八	Bā	Eight
九	Jyòu	Nine
十	Shŕ	Ten

NUMBER-MEASURE

For counting objects.

一 個	Yīge	One
兩 個	Lyǎngge	Two
三 個	Sānge	Three
四 個	Sz̀ge	Four
五 個	Wǔge	Five
六 個	Lyòuge	Six
七 個	Chīge	Seven
八 個	Bāge	Eight
九 個	Jyòuge	Nine
十 個	Shŕge	Ten

ELEVEN   SHŔ-YĪ   NUMBER

Eleven is ten-one. The rest of the
teens are composed in this way.

TWELVE	Shŕ-èr	十二
THIRTEEN	Shŕ-sān	十三
FOURTEEN	Shŕ-sż	十四
FIFTEEN	Shŕ-wǔ	十五
SIXTEEN	Shŕ-lyòu	十六
SEVENTEEN	Shŕ-chī	十七
EIGHTEEN	Shŕ-bā	十八
NINETEEN	Shŕ-jyòu	十九

TWENTY   ÈR-SHŔ   NUMBER

Twenty is two-tens. Thirty is three-
tens 三十 . Forty is four-tens
四十 .

TWENTY-ONE	二十一
THIRTY-SEVEN	二十二
FORTY-FIVE	二十三
SIXTY-EIGHT	二十四
NINETY-NINE	二十五

百

HUNDRED   BǍI   NUMBER

One hundred   yī bǎi   一 百
Two hundred   lyǎng bǎi   兩 百

一 丆 丆 𠂤 酉 百

千

THOUSAND   CHYÁN   NUMBER

One thousand   yī chyán   一 千
Nine thousand   jyǒu chyán   九 千

丿 二 千

萬

TEN THOUSAND   WÀN   NUMBER

English does not have a special name for tens of thousands, but Chinese does. Wǔ wàn 五 萬 is fifty thousand. For patterns, see Grammar Section.

丶 亠 艹 艹 艹 莒 苎 芮 苜 萬 蕈 萬 萬

HOW MANY?   JĬ   NUMBER

This question word is used before measures (only for numbers up to ten).

一個人   yīge rén   one man.

幾個人?   jĭge rén   how many men?

乙 幺 幺 糸 纟 纟 絲 絲 絲 絲 幾 幾 幾

THE MEASURE

GE   MEASURE

All expressions referring to a specific number of things
must use a measure in Chinese. This is the most general measure.
It is used with any noun that doesn't have a particular measure
of its own. The pattern is <u>Number Measure Noun</u>.

Example: 一個女人. yīge nyǔrén   one woman

(See Grammar Section for definition and more examples.)

ノ 亻 亻 们 们 俐 個 個 個 個

189

BĚN **MEASURE**

Used for books, magazines and other things which have bindings.

一 十 才 木 本

JĀNG **MEASURE**

For things having flat extended surfaces, such as tables, beds or paper.

⁊ ⁊ ⁊ ⁊⌐ ⁊⌐ ⁊⌐ ⁊⌐ 張 張 張 張

WÈI **MEASURE**

For persons, an indication of respect.

⼃ ⼂ ⼂' ⼂⁻ ⼂⁻ 位 位 位

SPECIFIERS

The equivalent of the English demonstrative pronouns, this and that. See Grammar Section for patterns.

這

THIS	JÈI	SPECIFIER

`、　一　亠　言　言　言　言　言`

`言　言　這`

THIS ONE　　JÈIGE　　SPECIFIER-MEASURE

This combination can modify a noun or stand alone as a pronoun.

這個

那個人高.　　　Jèige rén gāu.
　　　　　　　　This man is tall.

這個好.　　　　Jèige hǎu.
　　　　　　　　This is good.

那

THAT	NÈI	SPECIFIER

`フ　ヲ　习　月　刄ˊ　刄ˀ　那`

THAT ONE　　NÈIGE　　SPECIFIER-MEASURE

Also modifies a noun or stands alone as a pronoun.

那個

那個女人矮.　　　Nèige nyǔrén ǎi.
　　　　　　　　That woman is small.

我要那個.　　　Wǒ yàu nèige.
　　　　　　　　I want that.

WHICH?   NĚI   QUESTION-WORD/SPECIFIER

   This word is written the same as <u>nei</u>, with a small mouth
added at the left, but it is pronounced in the low tone. Use
it exactly the same as <u>jèi</u> or <u>nèi</u>.

丶 口 口 叮 叼 叼 哎 哎 哎 哪

哪 個

WHICH (ONE)?   NĚIGE   ADJECTIVE/PRONOUN

   Like <u>jèige</u> or <u>nèige</u>, this can stand alóne as a pronoun,
or modify a noun.

QUESTION WORDS

When one of these words replaces a noun in a sentence,
a question is formed. See Grammar Section.

WHO?   SHÉI   PRONOUN

Used as the subject or object of a sentence.

她是誰！   Tā shr̀ shéi?   Who is she?

誰去？   Shéi chyù?   Who is going?

WHAT?   SHEMMA   NOUN/ADJECTIVE

WHY?   WEISHÉMMA   ADVERB/QUESTION WORD

This word follows the subject, precedes the verb. It is
the equivalent of the French <u>pourquoi</u>, literally meaning,
"for what?"

你為什麼去? Nǐ weishémma chyù?   Why are you going?

VERBS

ADVERBS

CO-VERBS

POSTVERBS

LOCALIZERS

PARTICLES

THE VERB "TO BE"

TO BE   SHŔ   VERB

Shŕ is called an equative verb because it can act as an
equals sign between two nouns. Like the English verb <u>to be</u>,
it shows a state of being, and doesn't indicate action.

丨 丨丨 日 日 旦 早 早 是 是

TWO <u>COLLOQUIALISMS</u>:

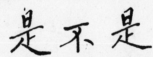

SHŔ-BÙ-SHŔ

If you make a statement, and you wish to know someone's
reaction, you say, shŕ-bù-shŕ. It's like saying "right?" in
English, "n'est-ce pas?" in French, or "verdad?" in Spanish.

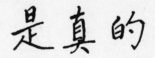

SHŔ-JĒN-DE

The reply. It means "Right!"

THE VERB "TO HAVE"

TO HAVE   YǑU   VERB

This is a drawing of a right hand and meat 舅 , radicals 29 and 130.

一 ナ オ 冇 有 有

没 有

NOT HAVE   MÉIYǑU   NEGATIVE-VERB

<u>Méi</u> 没 is a special negative for the verb <u>yǒu</u>, the only verb which never uses the standard negative <u>bù</u>.

丶 丶 氵 氵 氵 没 没

STATIVE VERBS

These verbs describe the state of someone or something.
In English, we use a form of the verb <u>to be</u> plus an adjective.
The food <u>is good</u>. The children <u>are beautiful</u>. Chinese stative
verbs have a self-contained <u>to be</u>. They are also used as
adjectives. The patterns are: <u>N SV</u> and <u>SV N</u>.

BIG   DÀ   STATIVE VERB/ADJECTIVE

A drawing of a man with his arms extended, indicating bigness.

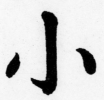

SMALL   SYǍU   STATIVE VERB/ADJECTIVE

Originally, three small dots (perhaps meaning three little
objects?).

A LOT   DWŌ   STATIVE VERB/ADJECTIVE

These are two drawings of <u>flesh</u>, which originally meant
<u>plentiful</u> <u>provisions</u>. An example of using a concrete object
to indicate an abstract idea. Translate "there are a lot of ____."

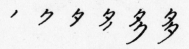

FEW   SHǍU   STATIVE VERB/ADJECTIVE

The derivation of this character is uncertain. It is <u>small</u>
with an extra stroke. The question word <u>How much?</u> is made of
多 <u>a lot</u> and 少 <u>a little</u>: dwōshǎu 多少.

丿 小 小 少

GOOD   HǍU   STATIVE VERB/ADJECTIVE

This is a picture of a woman with her child, which respresents goodness to the Chinese. In the classical language, this word can also mean <u>love</u>.

く　夕　女　女'　奵　好

BAD   HWÀI   STATIVE VERB/ADJECTIVE

一　十　士　圠　圠　圠　圿　坮　坮　坢　坤　坤
塻　塻　塻　壃　壊　壞　壞

NEW   **SYĪN**   **STATIVE VERB/ADJECTIVE**

丶 亠 六 宁 立 立 辛 辛 亲 亲 新 新 新

OLD   **JYÒU**   **STATIVE VERB/ADJECTIVE**

This word is used for old objects, such as <u>an old</u> <u>book</u>,
hen jyoude shu 很舊的書.

丶 艹 艹 苧 苧 荏 荏 萑 萑 萑 萑 舊 舊 舊

OLD   **LǍU**   **STATIVE VERB/ADJECTIVE**

This word is used for people, such as <u>an old</u> <u>woman</u>, hen
laude nyuren 很老的女人.

一 十 土 耂 耂 老

EARLY **DZǍU** **STATIVE VERB/ADJECTIVE**

This shows the sun coming up over the horizon 旦 , or dawn, the <u>early</u> part of the day.

｜ 冂 日 日 旦 早

ALL RIGHT **SYÍNG** **STATIVE VERB/ADJECTIVE**

A drawing of an intersection 㠁 . In ancient times, this word meant <u>street</u>.

丿 彳 彳 行 行 行

POLITE   KÈCHÌ   **STATIVE VERB/ADJECTIVE**

This means, "the air of a guest." A guest is someone with his feet 夂 and his mouth 口 under your roof 宀 .

謝 謝	Syè syè.	Thank you.
不 客 氣	Bù kèchì.	You're welcome. (don't be polite.)

丶 丷 宀 宀 宀 安 安 客 客

丶 厂 气 气 气 氕 氣 氣 氣

Position of Hand with Brush -- Lifted
(Laura DeCoppet)

Position of Hand with Brush -- Pressing
(Laura DeCoppet)

ADVERBS

Fixed adverbs <u>must</u> follow the subject. Moveable adverbs
can precede <u>or</u> follow the subject.

VERY   HĚN   FIXED ADVERB

Hen may only be used with stative verbs: very good, very
tall. 彳 is the radical and 艮 is the phonetic. 艮 is also
the phonetic in 跟 <u>gen</u>, "with."

ノ ノ 彳 彳 彳 彳 很 很 很 很

NOT   BÙ   FIXED ADVERB

Bu can be placed before any verb to negate the meaning of
the sentence. It is also used for the choice question.

他好.   He is good.   他不好. He is not good.

他來.   He is coming.   他不來. He is not coming.

一 フ 才 不

TOO, AND, ALSO   YĚ   **FIXED ADVERB**

Exactly like its English counterpart, except that it follows a specific word order. It must always appear after the subject and before the verb. This character is very ancient, a drawing of a snake. It was borrowed to write this word. A nice character to write because it has two hooks.

乙 乜 也

ALL   DŌU   **FIXED ADVERB**

一 十 土 耂 耂 者 者 者 者 者 者 都

MOST   DZWÈI   ADVERB

   This is the superlative in Chinese and is equivalent the
the English -est, as in hungriest, fastest. It is used before
a stative verb or an adjective.

   这個最好.   Jèige dzwèi hǎu.   This is the best.

ㄧ 冂 日 日 旦 早 早 昻 昻 昻 最 最

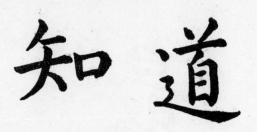

TO KNOW   JR̆DĂU   VERB

   This word is composed of two synonyms. A man beside a mouth
for the first character. A head on a path for the second.

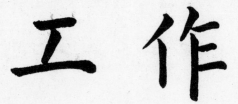

TO WORK   GŪNGDZWÒ   VERB

Another synonym compound. This word can also be a noun.

VERB-OBJECT COMPOUNDS

TO READ   KÀNSHŪ   VERB-OBJECT

Literally, "see book." The word <u>see</u> is an eye 目 and a hand 手, the object of perception. <u>Book</u> shows a hand holding a writing brush and a phonetic 曰.

TO STUDY   NYÀNSHŪ   VERB-OBJECT

If there is a particular object, it can replace the general object. To study Chinese, nyán jūnggwó hwà, 念中國話

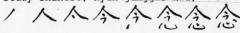

說 話

TO SPEAK   **SHWŌHWÀ**   **VERB-OBJECT**

The <u>word</u> or <u>speech</u> radical appears in both words: 言.

寫 字

TO WRITE   **SYĚDZ̀**   **VERB-OBJECT**

Literally, <u>to write</u> characters. Dz̀ is <u>character</u>.

TO EAT   **CHRFÀN**   **VERB-OBJECT**

This literally means <u>eat-food</u>. Chr has the mouth radical 口 .
Fan is "a collection of victuals" with 스 "collection" and
艮 "pan and spoon." (Karlgren) You can chr <u>jūngqwó fàn</u>
(eat Chinese food), chr <u>měigwó fàn</u> (eat American food), chr
<u>fǎgwó fàn</u> (eat French food).

ㄧ 口 口 叫 吖 吃
丿 亻 亽 今 今 全 食 食 食 飠 飯 飯

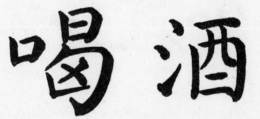

TO DRINK   **HÉJYǑU**   **VERB-OBJECT**

You can héchá (drink tea), hé tāng(eat soup). The mouth
radical 口 appears in <u>drink</u>, and the water radical 氵 in <u>wine</u>.

ㄧ 冂 口 口 叩 呾 吗 昆 喝 喝 喝 喝
丶 冫 氵 汀 沂 沔 洒 洒 酒 酒

TO PAINT   HWÀ HWÀR   VERB-OBJECT

    This is an example of the same word used first as a verb,
then as a noun (as object of the verb). In English this would
be a redundancy, "to paint a painting." The character is a
picture of a hand and writing brush making a drawing 畫 .

| TO SING | CHÀNGGĒR | VERB-OBJECT |

Literally, <u>to sing a song</u>. The third character is a diminutive, a characteristic decoration of Peking Mandarin speech. This final <u>r</u> sound occurs frequently. The character is a drawing of a child 兒.

走 路

TO WALK, LEAVE　　　　　DZǑULÙ　　　　VERB-OBJECT

一 十 土 キ キ 走 走

丶 口 口 呆 呆 足 足 趵 趵 政 路 路 路

做 事

TO WORK　　　　　　DZWÒSHR　　　　VERB-OBJECT

To cook is dzwòfàn. 做飯.

丿 亻 亻 什 什 估 估 做 做 做 做

一 丁 丙 百 写 寻 寻 事

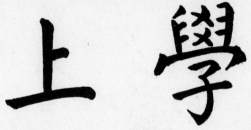

TO GO TO SCHOOL SHĀNGSYWÉ **VERB-OBJECT**

Shang can be an action verb as well as a localizer and a stative verb.

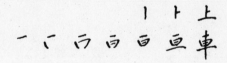

TO GET INTO A CAR SHĀNGCHĒ **VERB-OBJECT**

THE AUXILIARY VERB

A special use of the full verb.

TO LIKE, LOVE   AÌ   AUXILIARY VERB, VERB

The Chinese word functions like the English word: an auxiliary (I <u>like</u> to study), and a full verb (I <u>love</u> her).

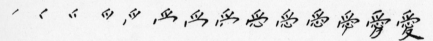

TO WANT   YÀU   AUXILIARY VERB, VERB

Full verb: I want that book.   我要那本書.

Auxiliary verb: I want to study.   我要念書.

MUST, HAVE TO   DĚI   AUXILIARY VERB, VERB

As a full verb, this word means <u>to obtain</u>. It shows a hand holding a cowrie shell (used for money) . The left part was added much later.

KNOW HOW   HWĚI   AUXILIARY VERB, VERB

As a full verb, this word means <u>meet</u>. It shows a covered pot with all the contents inside. As an auxiliary verb, it means <u>know how</u>, as in "I know how to sing."

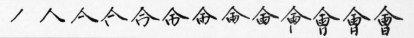

BE ABLE TO   NÉNG   AUXILIARY VERB

    The ancient drawing was a bear, a symbol meaning <u>powerful</u> which is directly related to the modern meaning.

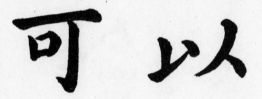

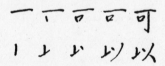

CAN   KÉYĬ   AUXILIARY VERB

一　丆　口　口　可

丨　以　以　以　以

CO-VERBS

These are Chinese prepositions. Unlike English prepositions
which may be attached to a sentence almost anywhere, co-verbs
have a fixed place in Chinese word order: <u>N   CV   O   V</u> .

WITH   GĒN   CO-VERB

跟 is the phonetic, the same phonetic in 很 hěn, <u>very</u>.

足 is a man walking, which means <u>follow</u>.

你跟我走嗎! Nǐ gēn wó dzǒu ma?   Will you walk with me?

丶 丨冂 凵 曱 甼 昗 足 趴 跀 跀 跟 跟 跟

TO, FOR   GĚI   CO-VERB

This is the preposition used for indirect objects. First
the indirect object following <u>gei</u>, then the direct object.

給他錢. Gěi tā chyán.   Give him money.

ㄥ ㄠ ㄠ ㄠ ㄠ ㄠ ㄠ ㄠ 約 約 給 給 給

TO   DWÈI   CO-VERB

This co-verb is used with the verb <u>speak</u>. It literally
means <u>facing</u>. The English sentence "I'm speaking to you"
translates, "I face you (and) speak."

ㅣ ㅣㅣ ㅓㅓ ㅓㅓ 业 非 非 业 业 業 業 業 對 對

TO BE IN, AT   DZÀI   CO-VERB

The drawing shows timber (phonetic) <u>on</u> the earth 土 .
This co-verb takes as its object a place-word or a noun with
a localizer (jyālǐ 家裡 , in the house).

一 大 才 才 在 在

這 兒

HERE   JÈR   PLACE-WORD

The specifier <u>jèi</u> with the diminutive <u>er</u> is a place-word
and may follow <u>dzài</u>.

那 兒

THERE   NÈR   PLACE-WORD

The same idea. He is over there, tā dzài nèr. 他在那兒.

POST-VERBS

These are prepositions which can follow the verb. See
Grammar Section.

TO BE IN, AT, ON   DZÀI   POST-VERB

Dzài can follow a verb indicating location. It is followed
by a place-word.

住 在

TO LIVE AT, IN   JÙ DZÀI   VERB POST-VERB

我住在美國.   Wǒ judzài Měigwó.   I live in America.

坐 在

TO SIT DOWN   DZWÒ DZÀI   VERB POST-VERB

請坐在這兒.   Chǐng dzwò dzài jèr.   Please sit down here.

TO   DÀU   POST-VERB

This <u>to</u> indicates arrival at a destination or a time.
The ancient graph shows a bird flying downward <u>reaching</u> 至
the ground. Knife 刂 is the phonetic here.

一 工 乙 玉 平 至 到 到

去 到

GO TO   CHYÙ DÀU   VERB POST-VERB

This combination can take a place-word or a time-word. If
a time-word, the phrase would translate, "go until _____."

走 到

WALK TO   DZǑU DÀU   VERB POST-VERB

THE LOCALIZER

A noun followed by a localizer becomes a place-word. Then
this place-word can be the object of a co-verb or a post-verb.

IN 他在學校裡.	LǏ	LOCALIZER
他在飯館裡.	Tā dzài sywésyàulǐ.	She is in school.
	Tā dzài fàngwárlǐ.	He is in the restaurant.

ˋ 尸 ㇁ 衤 衤 礻 初 袇 袒 袒 裡 裡

OUT   WÀI   LOCALIZER

卜 , a picture of a divining rod, means <u>prognosticate</u>.
夕 is the phonetic.

他在門外.   Tā dzài ménwài.   She is outside the door.

ㄧ ㄆ ㄓ 夕 ㄗ 外

ON, ABOVE   SHĀNG   LOCALIZER, VERB

    This character is an abstract symbol showing one line <u>above</u>
another. The book is on the table. 書在桌子上.
Shū dzài jwōdzshàng.

BELOW, BENEATH   SYÀ   LOCALIZER, VERB

    One line <u>beneath</u> another, a picture of the relationship.
The book is under the table. 書在桌子下.   Shū
dzài jwòdzsyà.

LEFT   DZWŎ   LOCALIZER

The drawing is a left hand holding a carpenter's square 左.
It means <u>work</u>.

一 ナ 左 左 左

RIGHT   YÒU   LOCALIZER

The drawing is a right hand and a mouth 右 , possibly
meaning <u>to eat</u>.

一 ナ 大 右 右

VERBS OF MOTION

These verbs have special patterns and special co-verbs.
See Grammar Section.

TO COME   LÁI   VERB

This is a drawing of wheat. It was borrowed to write
<u>come</u> because both words <u>pronounced</u> the same in ancient Chinese.

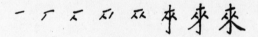

TO GO   CHYÙ   VERB

The ancient drawing showed a man with a ball between his
legs, 夳 , possibly meaning <u>to</u> <u>castrate</u>, a variation of the
fundamental meaning, <u>to remove</u>, <u>to take</u> <u>away</u>.

WITH THEIR CO-VERBS

These may be used separately, together, or in any combination, but in this order. For patterns, see Grammar Section.

BY   DZWÒ   CO-VERB

The name of some means of transportation follows this co-verb. It is a drawing of two men, very small, sitting on a big earth. As a full verb, this character means <u>to sit</u>.

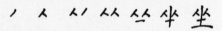

FROM   TSÚNG   CO-VERB

The original meaning of this word was <u>to follow</u>. The left side is a footprint. The right side shows two men, one behind the other, with <u>walking</u> below. A placeword must follow this character.

TO   DÀU   CO-VERB

As stated previously, the right side gives the sound of this word and the left side shows a bird flying downward 至, reaching the earth. Thus, the modern meaning, to arrive at. This co-verb takes a place-word as an object.

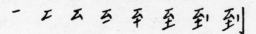

THE PARTICLE

THE CHINESE QUESTION MARK   MA   PARTICLE

This word performs the same function as the English question mark and occupies exactly the same position in the sentence. Place it at the end of any statement, and the statement becomes a question. (See Grammar Section.)

Horse is the phonetic (the right part, pronouncing ma) and the mouth radical (#30) is the sense-indicator. The word has a neutral tone.

LE   PARTICLE

When this particle follows a verb, it indicates the past
tense, completed action. It has a neutral tone. Used with a
verb-object compound, it may follow either the verb or the object.

YÀU   PARTICLE

This precedes the verb and indicates the future, exactly
like the English word "will."

我要去.   Wǒ yàu chyù.   I will go.

一　厂　冂　西　西　西　要　要　要

BIBLIOGRAPHY

BACKGROUND

Creel, H. G. Chinese Thought from Confucius to Mao Tse-tung.
    Reference on Philosophy

deBary, William T, ed. Sources of Chinese Tradition, 2 vols.
    New York: Columbia University Press, Reference on
    Philosophy

Yu-Lan, Feng. A Short History of Chinese Philosophy. New York:
    Free Press.

Payne, Robert, ed. The White Pony: An Anthology of Chinese
    Poetry. New York: New American Library, 1947.

Wallnofer and Rottauscher. Chinese Folk Medicine. New York:
    Bell Publishing Co., 1965. Cycle of Five Elements.

CALLIGRAPHY

Burdley, Michael. The Chinese Collector through the Centuries.
    Rutland, Vt.: Charles E. Tuttle Co., 1966.

Willetts, William. Foundations of Chinese Art. New York:
    McGraw-Hill, 1965.

Yee, Chiang. Chinese Calligraphy: An Introduction to Its
    Aesthetic and Technique, 3d ed. Cambridge, Mass.:
    Harvard University Press, 1973. The source most heavily
    relied on for information in Chapter 8. A beautiful book.

DICTIONARIES

Mathews, R.H. Mathews' Chinese-English Dictionary, rev. ed.
    Cambridge, Mass.: Harvard University Press, 1965.

Institute of Far Eastern Languages, Yale University.
    Dictionary of Spoken Chinese. New Haven, Conn.: Yale
    University Press, 1948.

ETYMOLOGIES AND LANGUAGE HISTORY

Karlgren, Bernhard, without whose extensive and brilliant
    work this book would have been impossible.

    Analytic Dictionary of Chinese and Sino-Japanese.
    Tai Pai, Taiwan: Cheng Wen Publishing Co., 1966.

Easy Lessons in Chinese Writing. Stockholm: Naturometodens Sprakinstitut, 1958.

Grammata Serica Recensa. Stockholm: Museum of Far Antiquities Bulletin No. 29, 1957.

Sound and Symbol in Chinese. London: Oxford University Press, 1962.

PATTERNS

Tewksbury, M. Gardner. _Speak Chinese_. New Haven, Conn.: Far Eastern Publications, Yale University, 1948.

Speak Chinese, rev. ed., Lessons 1-6. New Haven, Conn.: Far Eastern Language Publications, Yale University Press, n.d.

ORIENTAL BOOKSTORES

Orientalia, 61 Fourth Avenue, New York, N.Y.   10003.

Paragon, 14 East 38th Street, New York, N.Y.   10017.

Samuel Weiser, Inc., 734 Broadway, New York, N.Y.